THIS IS A PRION BOOK

Design copyright © 2007 Carlton Books Ltd
Text copyright © 2007 Carlton Books Ltd

Published in 2007 by Prion
An imprint of the Carlton Publishing Group
20 Mortimer Street
London W1T 3JW

10 9 8 7 6 5 4 3 2 1

A CIP catalogue entry for this book is available from the British Library.

ISBN 978 1 85375 632 0

Art Direction: Gülen Shevki-Taylor
Designer: Vicky Rankin
Project Editor: Gareth Jones
Artwork: Peter Liddiard
Production: Lisa Moore

Printed in Dubai

The Outdoor Book for Adventurous Chaps

ESSENTIAL SKILLS AND ACTIVITIES FOR BOYS OF ALL AGES

WRITTEN BY ADRIAN BESLEY

ILLUSTRATIONS BY PETER LIDDIARD

PRION

CONTENTS

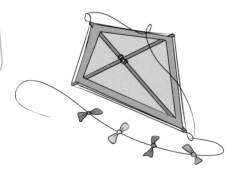

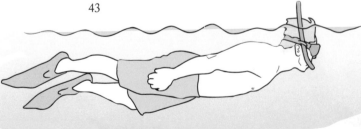

WILDERNESS SURVIVAL

CUNNING INVENTIONS

EXTREME SURVIVAL

INTRODUCTION

THE outdoors. It used to be all around us – a short cycle ride or a brisk stroll would bring us to fields of fun, adventure and derring-do. These days, it isn't always so easy: the urban sprawl seems to have taken the outdoors further and further away and the leisure alternatives – television, video games, the Internet – often provide more convenient pursuits.

Yet, the adventurous chap is made of sterner stuff and always finds a way. A back yard, a day out fishing, a camping trip or a beach holiday – all offer opportunities for excitement and exhilaration. This book is for the adventurous chap in us all: from the novice camper who has yet to light his first campfire to the seasoned adventurer seeking to survive in the wilderness. And, of course, it is also for those who are happy to dream and plan, lying on the sofa in front of the TV.

The ideas listed in the book are wide and varied and are aimed to inspire your adventures in the outdoors. Some are straightforward, others require more forethought; some can help you enjoy your surroundings while others may just save you from a potentially dangerous situation; there are games, skills, projects and guides, but they all share one basic theme: the outdoors is fun, exciting and more accessible than you could ever have thought.

WARNING

This book has been designed as an entertaining and nostalgic insight into the outdoors. Its contents have been selected and adapted by the author for amusement and interest, and are not intended to be prescriptive or to be taken literally. The reader should not treat the book as being a genuine book of advice. Some instructions are dangerous and must not be followed - for instance do not go anywhere near a crocodile. Neither the author nor the publisher accepts responsibility for, or shall be liable for, any accident, injury, loss or damage (including any consequential loss) that a reader may suffer after using the ideas, information, procedures or advice offered in this book.

WHAT TO WEAR FOR AN OUTDOOR ADVENTURE

PACKING and wearing the correct clothing is essential for any outdoor trip. Whether it's a short hike, a weekend camping expedition or a long journey, the maxim is the same: prepare for every eventuality. The most efficient method of packing for a wide range of climates is to select clothes that can be mixed and matched. If you cover the four basic categories – inner layer, mid-layer, insulation layer and outer layer – you will find you're prepared for almost all weather conditions.

INNER LAYER

Inner-layer clothing is worn next to your skin. It provides important insulation and is essential for wicking the sweat from your skin during energetic activities, so you stay comfortable without being damp. Everyday cotton inner-layer clothing might be comfortable, but it absorbs sweat and doesn't dry easily, so it might be worth looking at garments made from specialist materials such as polypropylene, which are designed to be lightweight, warm and efficient at allowing sweat to evaporate.

MID-LAYER

Over the inner layer you should wear your comfortable everyday clothes – T-shirts, long-sleeve shirts and shorts or trousers. Be sensible about your choice. Is your favourite shirt a little too tight? Will those trousers dry quickly enough if you're caught in a rainstorm? The comfort and lightness of cotton makes it a popular choice, but, once again, an investment in specialist clothing can pay dividends.

INSULATION LAYER

If the weather is likely to become cold, even if only at night, you will need sweatshirts, jumpers, jackets, hats and gloves. However, beware, because these can become a burden, so the best items are not only warm, but also lightweight and they 'breathe' to let sweat and excess body heat escape too. Wool is the traditional option, but now pile, fleece and wind-proof materials provide further choices.

OUTER LAYER

These are the clothes – jackets and overtrousers – that will protect you from the wind, rain and snow. Again, the best items, made from materials such as Gore-Tex®, are breathable. However, they are expensive, so waterproof PVC may be a more economic alternative. Other considerations are whether the neck and cuffs fasten to provide added protection in bad weather, whether there is a hood and whether the garment has sufficient pockets.

THE ADVENTURER'S BEST FRIENDS: HIS BOOTS!

There is one element of your attire that must be given much more consideration than anything else – your footwear. First, choose the right socks: wear a thin, wicking liner sock underneath a well-fitting, wool-rich sock to provide padding and cushioning. Then, select your footwear according to what you propose to do. Everyday trainers (sneakers) can be ideal for a day-trip; sandals are fine in the summer and are suitable for resting your feet at camp or for crossing a river; hiking shoes are tougher and offer more support for longer or multi-day hikes and walking or hiking boots, which often have toe caps and sweat-wicking lining, are especially designed for more rugged terrain.

HOW TO PREDICT THE WEATHER

THE good outdoorsman will always have one eye on the sky, because by observing and interpreting the formations of clouds overhead, it is entirely possible for the casual watcher to forecast the weather over the coming hours and days.

TYPES OF CLOUD

Cirrus clouds: the word 'cirrus' means 'curl' or 'fringe'. These clouds are thin, wispy and extremely high up in the atmosphere. If they start to join up or drop in height then it may rain within two days. Similarly, if they do not change, staying thin and wispy, then it would be a fair assumption that it will stay dry.

Stratus clouds: this type of cloud has no real defined base or top, hence the name 'stratus', meaning 'spread over area'. It tends to appear as a sheet of cloud, covering part of the sky. There are three notable classifications:

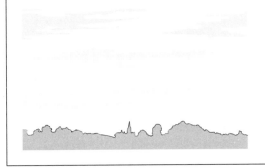

- Cirrostratus are extremely high-level, layered clouds. Often forming halos around the sun and moon, they can be a sign of rain in the coming days.

- Altostratus are mid-level, flat clouds, often dark grey in colour and in darkening skies are often a sign of rain.

- Nimbostratus are dark, overbearing, low-level, rain-bearing clouds that can give rise to persistent precipitation.

Cumulus clouds: these are fluffy, cotton wool-style clouds (cumulus means 'heap' or 'pile'). There are six major types of cumulus cloud:

- Cirrocumulus are high-level clouds often embedded within blankets of cirrus clouds and are a good indication of changing weather.
- Altocumulus are usually formed at a mid-level. If they are whipping around the sky, normally from west to north-west, it is quite possible that there will be a hard and heavy rain- or hailstorm very soon.

- Cumulonimbus are massive, towering, anvil-shaped clouds, usually associated with heavy rainshowers, hail and thunder and lightning.
- Fair-weather cumulus are low-level clouds resembling clumps of cotton wool.
- Swelling cumulus resemble cauliflower heads and are usually formed at mid-level. These clouds are a sign of instability and can often turn into rain-bearing clouds.
- Cumulus congestus are high-level clouds with a top more like traditional fair-weather cumulus rather than the anvil shape of cumulonimbus.

SIGNS OF BAD WEATHER

- The sun rises over a bank of clouds – indicates windy weather.
- Rolled- or jagged-edged clouds – indicate strong winds.
- Clouds racing across the sky, beginning to get fuller and blacker – indicate possible heavy rain.
- Clouds moving in all directions – indicate extreme instability.
- It's a hot day and clouds begin to grow in early to mid-afternoon – indicate rain and possibly thunder later that evening.

SIGNS OF GOOD WEATHER

- Fog disappears and is replaced by clear skies by mid-morning, or early afternoon.
- Red skies at night indicate a fine day to follow
- Dew and fog in the early morning indicates good weather
- If the cloud base height is rising, and holes begin to appear in the covering, the weather is set to improve.
- If cumulus clouds do not develop until into the afternoon, expect continued fair weather.

SEVERE WEATHER WARNING!

If cumulonimbus clouds form fierce black bases and suddenly an unusual lightbulb-shaped protuberance appears at the bottom of one, run for cover – a tornado could be on its way.

STAR SPOTTING

THE night sky is a fascinating arena with so many intriguing and beautiful sights, from stars and constellations to planets and comets. About 6,000–8,000 stars are visible to the naked eye, but how do you make head or tail of them?

BIG DIPPER AND POLE STAR

The Big Dipper, also known as the Plough, is visible in northern skies all year round and is one of the most easily-recognizable groups of stars in the sky. In fact, it's our guide around the stars.

Look in the northern sky and try to find the handle. The arc of the handle should stand out and, once you've found the handle, finding the bowl is easy. Imagine a line connecting the two stars at the front of the bowl, continue for a distance five times that between the two stars and you'll arrive at the Pole Star. This stays in the same place throughout the course of every night and no matter where you are in the northern hemisphere, when you face the Pole Star you will be facing north.

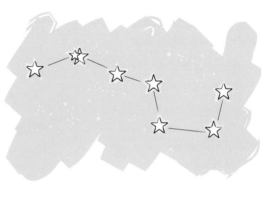

CASSIOPEIA

If you continue on this line past the Pole Star, at an equal distance opposite the Big Dipper, you'll find Cassiopeia; a W-shaped constellation floating in the starry band of the Milky Way.

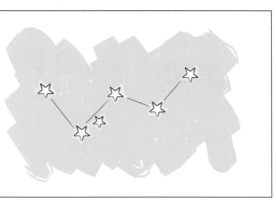

SOUTHERN CROSS

If you are in Australia or elsewhere in the southern hemisphere, two very bright stars can be seen quite near the horizon, one roughly above the other. These are, from the top, Beta Centauri and Alpha Centauri, and they point towards the Southern Cross. By drawing a line from Alpha through Beta and continuing up a very short distance you'll find the Cross, lying on its left side. The Southern Cross points south, so if you draw a line past the long stem of the cross for a distance of about three times its length, the point you hit will be about due south.

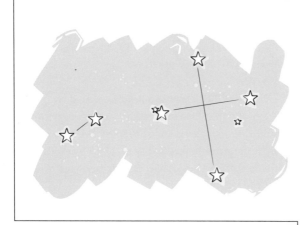

ORION

This group of stars resembles a man wearing a sword and belt. It is easily recognized by the three stars in a line – which form the belt – and three smaller stars in another line close by, which are the sword.

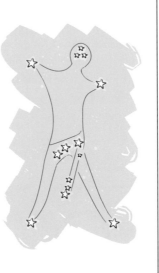

DOG STAR

To find the Dog Star, also known as Sirius, in the constellation Canis Minor, locate the belt of Orion. Connect a line through the three stars towards the horizon. This line will point to the Dog Star, which is the brightest star in the night sky and is often mistaken for a UFO!

RIDING YOUR BIKE OFF-ROAD

IS that the call of the wild? It's time to get the bike out of the garage and head for a muddy, adrenaline-fuelled off-road adventure…. Before you go, dress for the occasion – avoid baggy clothes and wear a helmet, a brightly-coloured garment, padded shorts, gloves and stiff-soled shoes. You should also prepare your bike. Oil the chain and check the gears, brakes and tyres. Don't overinflate your tyres if you're riding off-road as lower pressures, in the 35–45 psi range, will increase your control and comfort while improving traction and handling.

BOWLING ALONG

On your bike, you should aim to maximize the following:

Efficiency: control your gears to ride a full turn of the pedals every second. If you encounter a head wind or an incline then lower your gear to maintain your rhythm.

Power: make sure your knee is directly over the pedal. At the top of the pedal stroke (12 o'clock) you should be moving the pedal forwards; at the bottom (6 o'clock), move the pedal backwards. The only time you should be pushing directly down on the pedal is exactly at the halfway point between the top and the bottom (3 o'clock).

Comfort: bend your arms and keep an angle of about 90 degrees between your upper and lower arms, but stay relaxed. Grip the handlebars firmly, but not so tightly that your knuckles are white. Keep your back straight and at about 45 degrees to the ground. Sit on the saddle, but place some of your weight on the pedals, too.

RIDING UPHILL

Let your bodyweight press the pedal down while you pull up and back on the handlebars. As the hill gets steeper or you get tired, you will have to shift to lower gears to maintain your pedalling rhythm. Standing requires more effort, but can be effective for short, steep climbs.

RIDING DOWNHILL

Pick your route carefully, looking out for tree roots, stumps, puddles, loose gravel and ruts. Keep your pedals horizontal and transfer your weight to the back of the saddle. Your hands should stay on the brakes, squeezing the rear brake to keep control and using the front brake as support.

BUNNY HOPS

If you encounter a smallish obstacle you cannot avoid, you can try 'jumping' over it. To do this, approach the object at a jogging speed, gripping the pedals as tightly as possible with your toes. Compress your body by bending your knees, crouching and pushing down on your handlebars. When you reach the obstacle, 'explode' and push your whole body upwards, using your feet to pull the pedals and the back wheel up.

BUILDING A TREEHOUSE

NESTLED amid the branches and leaves of a huge tree, the treehouse is the perfect hideaway – you can see everything, but no one can see you. Whether it's a nature observation platform, a funhouse or a necessity for survival, you can design the ideal treehouse. Every tree is different and presents unique challenges to the treehouse-builder, but using this simple structure you should be able to construct your own magnificent hideout.

YOU WILL NEED

- Tree
- Ladder
- Lumber for frame
- Bolts
- Plywood for roof, floors and walls
- Saw
- Nails
- Hammer
- Drill
- Rope ladder and hooks

1. Your treehouse can be built on a single tree or between two or more trees. When selecting a suitable tree/s, ensure the tree is mature and healthy, and has a near vertical trunk of at least 30 cm (12 in) in width. Oak, beech, maple and fir trees are particularly suitable. Check the branches – are there enough emerging at right angles from the trunk? Are they strong enough to bear the weight of the house? Look for at least one or two of your supporting branches to be around 20 cm (8 in) thick.

2. Take a piece of paper and sketch out your house. Try to keep it as simple as possible. Now look at your tree and imagine where it will sit. The treehouse should be sited in the lower third of the tree, around 2.5 m (8 ft) from the ground, and ideally it should

be centred around the trunk, with as many branches as possible to support it. Finally, consider if there is sufficient space for your treehouse and whether some branches might need to be pruned.

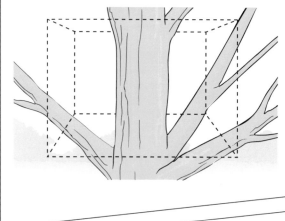

3. The base frame of your treehouse needs to be as secure as possible. Do this by connecting the supporting branches. Try to keep the base frame level and connect the branches with as few lengths of wood as you can. Using 15 cm (6 in) galvanized bolts, secure the frame to the branches. Before you continue, it is vitally important to ensure this part of the treehouse is completely

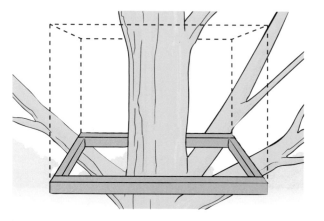

stable and able to bear weight. Carefully check each correction and ensure the frame does not wobble.

4. If any of the frame's sides remain unsupported by branches you should construct your own supports. Try running posts diagonally down to the trunk and securing them with a crossbeam.

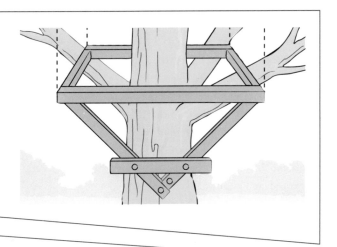

5. It may be easier to prepare the floor on the ground. Carefully measure the floor area of the frame and saw an equivalent-sized piece of plywood at least 2 cm (¾ in) thick. Cut out any holes necessary for protruding branches or tree trunks and make a doorway large enough for you to crawl through. If you need to, cut the floor into two or three sections so that they are easy to carry. Nail the floor to the base frame.

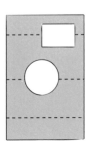 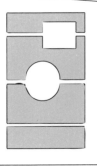

6. Position the wall and roof struts. The wall struts need to be around 2 m (6 ft 6 in) high at the back and around 30 cm (12 in) lower at the front. You will need an extra roof strut directly over the doorway.

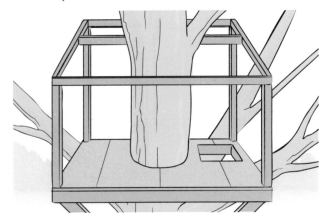

TREE CARE

Building a treehouse should do negligible or no harm to the tree, but it is important to bear in mind you're dealing with a living, growing part of the natural world. The tree will grow around your house, which might affect the fixings of your structure, and branches may grow and push through or around the house. When using nails or bolts to fix the treehouse to the tree, use as few as possible and site them as far apart as possible.

7. Once again return to the ground to prepare the walls and roof of the treehouse according to the measurements of your frame. Cut out any windows you require in the walls and, as you did with the floor, cut the walls into sections if it's difficult to carry them up in one piece to the house, then nail them to the frame. Cut the roof into sections to fit round the tree. Nail the roof to the walls as securely and snugly as possible.

8. Screw the hooks for your rope ladder to the extra roof strut, so that the ladder will drop through the door. This will enable you to climb all the way into the house rather than having to scramble up to the door.

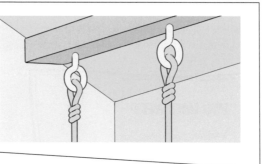

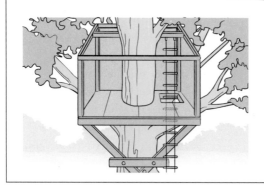

9. Fix the top of the ladder to the hooks, making sure that it is safely and securely attached. Return to ground level and test it can take your weight before climbing right up to the house. Each time you use the ladder, give it a good tug first to check that it's still safe to use.

HOW TO MAKE A ROPE SWING

BOY or man, there is something within us that loves to swing. Maybe it's our primeval jungle roots or perhaps just the influence of too many Tarzan films in our youth. The best swings hang from branches that lie across a bank or a steep slope, but if you can engineer it so that your swing flies out over a stream or river you have the added jeopardy of a soaking should you not complete the ride!

YOU WILL NEED

- Mature tree with sturdy, spreading branches
- Rope at least 2.5 cm (1 in) in diameter
- Ball of string
- Small heavy object – stone, cricket ball, spanner

1. The branch you select must be strong and healthy. If possible, choose a straight one that forms an L-shape, not a V, with the trunk. It should be at least 20 cm (8 in) in diameter at the point where you're going to attach the swing and 3–4 m (10–13 ft) off the ground.
2. Take a rough measurement from the branch to the point where you want the swing to hang to, then add about 3 m (10 ft) for loops and knots. If the rope has previously been cut you will find that it will have frayed; bind it with adhesive tape or melt the end over a flame for a few seconds.

3. Unravel your string so it lies loose and untangled on the ground. Tie one end of the string tightly to a small heavy object – a stone, a cricket ball, a spanner. Holding the tail end of the string firmly, throw the object over up the branch, so that it falls on the other side of it. Untie the object and tie one end of the rope to this end of the string. Holding on to the

other end of the rope, slowly and carefully use the string to pull the head of the rope up and over the branch, then down the other side. Untie the string and with the two ends of the rope fasten a timber hitch knot (see page 94) continuing to tighten until the knot has secured one end of the rope around the branch. Now you have your rope attached to the branch, you can choose which type of swing you want.

MAKING A LOOP SWING

Form a large loop in the hanging end of the rope using a bowline knot (see page 95). You can now stand or sit in the loop. Try winding yourself around and letting the swing spin you back.

MAKING A TARZAN SWING

Tie a short piece of wood to the tail of the rope, or just make a large enough knot at the bottom so that you can stand up on it and cry 'Aaaaaaah Ayaaaaahhh!'

MAKING CAMP

WHEN a fellow is nearing the end of a long trek or has stumbled upon an incredible vista, he will doubtless be tempted to set up his camp there and then. However, the sensible adventurer won't make a snap decision, but will carefully weigh up the pros and cons of any site in order to identify the perfect pitch.

THE ABSOLUTE ESSENTIALS

- Find a slightly elevated spot so that if there's a storm, rain will flow away from your tent, rather than under it.

- Make sure the ground is dry, but not so hard that it won't yield to a tent stake.

- Check around your intended site for potential rock falls, weak boughs or trees that look unsteady.

- Choose an area clear of rocks, branches or bumps. Remember, whatever is on the ground is what you'll be sleeping on.

- Check for animal tracks, droppings or bedding sites. The last thing you need is a bear visiting in the middle of the night.

IDEAL CONDITIONS

• Pick a site that has protection from driving wind and rain – large boulders, rock outcroppings or dense stands of trees form natural wind-blocks.

• Set your tent up so that the opening faces the wind, as this will greatly increase the ventilation in your tent and help you in your fight against condensation.

• If possible, orientate your tent door to the east or south-east to catch the morning sun. It will dry the tent out and warm you up.

• Find a dry, flat area for cooking, well away from any leaves or brush that may catch fire.

• Note the wind direction and ensure that flames and smoke will be blown away from the tent.

• Consider where you intend to find and store your wood and tinder.

• Check for a local water source – a stream, well or tap – as you're going to be making regular trips to it, returning with a heavy container.

PLACES TO AVOID

• Avoid areas known for avalanches and rock slides, and don't camp where a river might burst its banks.

• If you really need some shade, you can pitch your tent under trees, but not if there are high winds or it's likely to rain, and not under pine trees, which will drip sap or drop pine cones.

• Avoid tall, grassy meadows, as they are the natural habitat of ticks, ants and other bugs, and in rocky terrain beware of snake-infested ledges.

• Steer clear of areas heavy with mosquitoes and other insects. Mosquitoes like low, marshy places, still water, tall grass and bracken fern.

• Breezes blow up canyons or mountains during the day and down at night, while valleys and hollows are generally the wettest, coldest and foggiest spots.

PUTTING UP YOUR TENT

ANY chap with his wits about him can put up a tent, even in a force nine gale if necessary. If you follow the instructions closely, you'll have a dwelling that won't collapse or launch you into the air like a children's kite. Having selected the ideal spot to pitch your tent (see pages 24–25) take the tent out of its bag, placing the peg bag and other small equipment on top of the tent bag, so it doesn't blow away.

1. Decide the exact position of the tent, including which way the entrance is to face. Brush away any sticks, stones or detritus from the area.

2. Lie the tent out in its exact position. Peg out the tent. Put pegs in the front two corners first, then in the back two corners, then add the rest of the pegs. Make sure that the sides of the tent are fully stretched out.

3. Unfold all the poles and connect them together. Most frame tents have spring-loaded poles or a simple colour-coded system to indicate which poles fit together.

4. Lie the poles out on the ground in the pattern that they fit together. Lie the legs of the tent next to where they will go. If the legs come in more

than one piece don't worry about putting them together yet. Starting from the centre, or ridge, of the tent, connect the poles up.

5. Push the poles slightly into the ground at the front of the tent, then at the back.

6. Lay your ridge pole across the middle of the tent (you may need to slide it through some canvas loops). Remember not to walk on the tent or drag the poles across the tent. Hang the middle of the tent from the ridge pole.

7. Now put the fly sheet on. Take care not to rip the material on the two spikes at either end of the tent. Clip the sides of the inner and fly sheet together.
8. Peg out the fly sheet, pushing the pegs in at an angle of 45 degrees. Peg down the front two corners, then the back two corners, then the rest of the tent. Make sure you pull the tent's sides straight, because they should not flop around. It's important that the inner and fly sheet don't touch or rain will get in.

9. Tighten the main guys (you may need to peg these out if you haven't done so already) so that the tent will stand unaided. Ensure that the uprights are vertical and that the ridge of the tent is straight.
10. Tie the doors up now. If you peg the tent out with the doors untied you may find yourself unable to close them later!
11. Peg out any guy lines that are left, starting with the corner ones. They should normally come out at an angle of 45 degrees to the tent, as this will help give the tent its shape.

CAMP FURNITURE

WITH imagination and some forethought, it is perfectly possible to equip yourself for a comfortable stay at camp with furnishings of your own making. Indeed, without burdening your pack with anything more than necessary, you can enjoy almost all the creature comforts of home!

YOU WILL NEED

BASIC TOOLS:
- Selection of branches
- Small saw
- Knife
- Hammer
- Handful of nails

CONSTRUCTING A CAMP BED:
- Large ferns and twigs
- Straw, grass and leaves for 'mattress'

BUILDING TABLE AND CHAIRS:
- Scrap wood
- Packing box or old fenceboards

CONSTRUCTING A CAMP BED:

1. Spend some time finding two straight branches at least 10 cm (4 in) in diameter and as long as you need the bed to be (your height, plus a little more for good measure). Trim away offshoots and leaves until the branches are as smooth as possible.

2. Scoop out two parallel trenches for the branches about 60 cm (2 ft) apart, so that the branches are held firm, but stand slightly proud of the ground.

3. Collect 30 or so small straight branches of about 2–3 cm (¾–1¼ in) in diameter and at least 60 cm (2 ft) long. Strip them clean of all but their bark and spread them evenly across the trench. Turning any knots or knobs downwards, nail the branches to the parallels.

4. For the bedhead, lay a 10 cm (4 in) diameter branch (perhaps one left over from cutting the parallels) across the head of the bed. Dig five or six smaller branches into the ground, bend them to a 45-degree angle and nail them to the head, as shown in the diagram.

5. Now find whatever soft materials you can to make your 'mattress'. Place some large, soft ferns or twigs lengthways over the bed and then use straw, grass or leaves to build it up until it is at least 15 cm (6 in) deep.

6. Place a rolled-up jacket or a plastic bag full of straw over the bed head for a pillow. Lie back and enjoy some well-earned sleep.

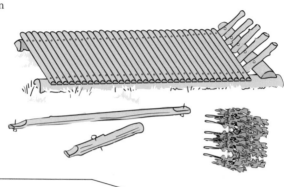

BUILDING A TABLE AND CHAIRS

Who wants to sit on hard or wet ground when, quickly and simply, you can put together a practical campsite table with seats?

1. Cut six pieces of wood around 75 cm (30 in) long. Nail together three of the pieces into an n-shape, then repeat with the other three.

2. Now cut the tabletop pieces. The length will depend on how many people you intend to sit at the table, but give each person at least 50 cm (20 in) of space, so if you're making a table for four, cut pieces 100 cm (3 ft 4 in) in length. Your table is 75 cm (30 in) wide, so you will need enough pieces to fill the tabletop, but don't worry about leaving gaps, as long as they're not wide enough for a cup to fall through.

3. Nail the tabletop pieces to join the legs of the table as shown in the diagram.

4. To construct the integral seating cut two 125-cm (50-in) pieces of wood and nail them across the legs at a height of about 45 cm (18 in) from the ground. Allow them to extend past the legs by equal lengths.

5. Secure the seats across these supports, remembering to make them slightly wider than the tabletop pieces. Take a seat and admire your handiwork – *bon appetit*!

BUILDING AND COOKING ON A CAMPFIRE

WARMTH, light and hot food – learn how to make an effective campfire and your life in the outdoors will suddenly become a whole lot easier

1. Situate your fire at least 3 m (10 ft) away from tents, trees, roots and anything else flammable. Clear a space approximately 100 cm (3 ft) square and dig out a small, shallow, keyhole-shaped pit in the ground. For safety and ease of use, the pit should be at least 25 cm (10 in) deep and the smaller end of the pit should be at least the circumference of your cooking utensil. Surround the smaller end of the pit with rocks, of a similar size if possible, so that a grille or old oven shelf can be placed evenly on top.

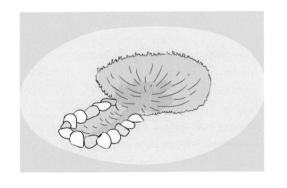

2. Gather dry firewood and kindling. For the best cooking coals, use hardwoods such as oak, cedar, mesquite and pecan, and avoid softwoods such as pine and aspen. On the main fire pit, build a small, loose pile of kindling, making sure to allow space for air to feed the fire. Construct a tepee of dry twigs and small sticks around and above the kindling pile.

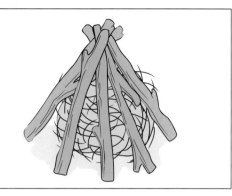

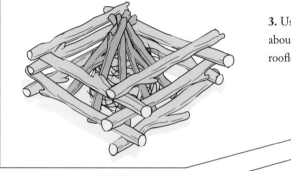

3. Using dry sticks and branches that are about 1.5 cm (½ in) in diameter, build a roofless cabin around the teepee.

4. Light the kindling with a match and add increasingly larger sticks and then logs as the fire grows in strength, always leaving enough space between them for the fire to breathe.

5. Let your fire burn for around 25 minutes until the flames and smoke have died down and the embers are glowing red. Then transfer a few hot embers to your smaller pit, which is the cooking area. Continue to keep the main fire burning and transfer hot embers over when those in the cooking pit have cooled.

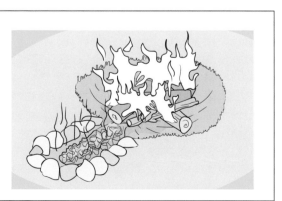

COOKING METHODS

Grilling: rest a grille or old oven shelf on large stones over the cooking pit.

Toasting: toast your food on long skewers held over the fire

On the coals: cook directly on the fire itself using larger stones to support your pot and to avoid extinguishing the fire. To prevent the pots becoming blackened with soot and ash, apply a layer of soap to the outside of the pot before cooking.

A rock grill: select a flat rock that is less than 5 cm (2 in) thick. Clean and dry it, and place it on the fire. Turn the rock over using a stick, allowing it to gradually heat on each side as evenly as possible. Place your food directly on the rock to cook it. When the upper surface cools, turn the rock over, brush it off and cook on the hot side.

CAMPFIRE SONGS

WHAT better way to pass the chilly evening hours than sitting around the campfire and enjoying a good old sing-song. Once you get everyone involved, it really does raise the spirits no matter how tiring the day has been. Don't be afraid to mix modern tunes – 'Meet the Flintstones', 'American Pie' or even a Scissor Sisters number – with the traditional songs listed here, just as long as everyone feels able to join in. And if there are actions to boot, well so much the better…

Start with this old favourite, to the tune of 'London's Burning':

Camp fire's burning, camp fire's burning,

Draw nearer, draw nearer,

In the glowing, in the glowing,

Come sing and be merry.

SWING LOW, SWEET CHARIOT

Now you're all warmed up, let's start the actions. Try singing the first chorus, adding the actions to the second and doing just actions for the third.

I looked over Jordan, and what did I see,
Comin' for to carry me home,
A band of angels coming after me,
Comin' for to carry me home.

Chorus:
Swing low, sweet chariot,
Comin' for to carry me home,
Swing low, sweet chariot,
Comin' for to carry me home.

If you get to heaven before I do,
Comin' for to carry me home,
Just tell all my friends that I'm a coming too,
Comin' for to carry me home.

[Chorus]

I'm sometimes up and sometimes down,
Comin' for to carry me home,
But still my soul feels heavenly bound,
Comin' for to carry me home.
[Chorus]

I've never been to heaven, but I've been told,
Comin' for to carry me home,
That the streets in heaven are paved with gold,
Comin' for to carry me home.
[Chorus]

Actions:
Swing – cradle an imaginary baby and gently swing
Low – place palms of hands on ground
Sweet – fingers to mouth tasting something good
Chariot – take hold of those reins and ride
Coming – beckon towards you
For – hold up four fingers
To – hold up two fingers
Carry – hold heavy weight above head
Me – point to yourself
Home – make roof above your head

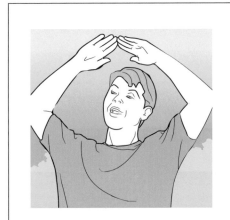

KUM BA YAH

Try making up your own verses and actions to match. For example, for 'Someone's camping, Lord' make a tent shape with outstretched arms.

Kum ba yah, my Lord, kum ba yah!
[repeat twice more]
Oh Lord, kum ba yah!

Someone's sleeping, Lord…

Someone's crying, Lord…

Someone's singing, Lord…

Someone's laughing, Lord…

Someone's camping, Lord…

Actions:
Kum ba yah – hand over hand, then arms out to either side
Lord – extend arms upward

AULD LANG SYNE

For the end of the last night of an expedition…

Should auld acquaintance be forgot
And never brought to mind?
Should auld acquaintance be forgot
And days of auld lang syne?

Chorus:
For auld lang syne, my friend,
For auld lang syne;
We'll take a cup of kindness yet,
For auld lang syn

And here's a hand, my trusty friend,
And give's a hand of thine,
We'll take a cup of kindness yet,
For auld lang syne.

[Chorus]

Actions:
Stand up and cross your arms, holding the hand of the person on either side of you. Shake both hands as you sing the chorus. For a rousing finale, repeat the last chorus at twice the speed.

GING GANG GOOLI

To get us going, here's a good rousing song that everyone should know:

Ging gang gooli gooli gooli gooli watcha,
Ging gang goo, ging gang goo. [repeat]
Heyla, heyla sheyla, heyla sheyla heyla ho. [repeat]

Shali walli, shali walli, shali walli, shali walli,
Oompah, Oompah, Oompah.

Sing this as a round, with one group continuing with the 'Oompahs' and another singing the song again from the beginning.

STORIES AROUND THE CAMPFIRE

EVER since we learnt how to rub two sticks together, men have swapped stories around the campfire. As darkness falls, we all edge towards the light and warmth, and the flames and burning embers create shapes and shadows to tease our imaginations. All that's left is for someone to come forward with a true adventure story, a gripping yarn or a ghostly tale that will leave you looking over your shoulder as you trek back to your tent.

ENSURE YOUR LISTENERS ARE READY

The meal and camp chores should be finished and any necessary conversations dealt with. Your audience should now be quiet, attentive and eager to hear the story.

DON'T READ

What makes the story special is the telling. Be animated, stand up if necessary and act parts out, and make eye contact with your audience. If you forget exactly how the story goes, just make it up.

KNOW YOUR ROUTE AND DESTINATION

Take a minute to work out the story for yourself. There's nothing more irritating than a storyteller who has to backtrack to fit in an important detail he's forgotten. Divide the story into a beginning, a middle and an end, and mentally note the points you need to make at each stage. The rest is all embroidery and embellishment – but that's the real art of the storyteller.

PERSONALIZE THE STORY

Even if you're retelling a classic urban myth, your audience will be much more interested if they think the story really happened to you or at least someone close to you. Involve people and places that you might share an interest in, as it all adds to the veracity of your tale.

SET THE SCENE

Take some time to draw your audience into the story. Make sure the main character is painted as roundly as possible, the setting is described in detail and the essence of the narrative – whether it's a shaggy dog story, a supernatural thriller or a tale of derring-do – is established. It's not just what you say, but the rhythm and tone of your voice that will reel in your fellow campers.

INTRODUCE COLOUR AND SURPRISE

No one wants to hear a dull, monotonous anecdote. Liven up your story with different voices (especially if you're capable of reproducing regional accents), animal noises or creaking doors and rattling gates. Also assess how your audience are reacting to the story and wrack up the tension by whispering or shouting at crucial moments.

SIGNAL THE ENDING AND END!

As you approach the climax of your story it should be very obvious. All the loose ends should be tied up and you should finish at the very point the story does. No matter how successful your performance, never let yourself be tempted into starting another, lesser story – 'A couple of years later I went back to Mexico...'. Save it for another night.

PLAYING TAG

If no one steps forward to tell a tale, let the whole camp tell it. One chap starts with a sentence or two and then the camper on his left has to continue, before passing the developing saga onwards. Agree when the story is to end and let the person who began it all make up the final sentence.

EXPLORING ROCKPOOLS

ROCKPOOLS are incredibly exciting places to poke around in. When the difference between high and low tide is at its peak, you can spend hours walking on the bottom of the sea. The most important thing in planning a rockpool trip is to schedule it for as low a tide as possible. As the tide goes out, most of the creatures go out with it, but some can't move and are left on the rocks. This is where the fascination begins…

Watch carefully and quietly – many seashore creatures are hard to spot and they will conceal themselves from view if they think you're a threat (which you might be). You'll make discoveries on top of rocks, in cracks and crevices, under stones, on seaweed and in rockpools. Remember that every tiny element of a rockpool is very important to the survival of one creature or another, so leave everything just as you found it.

ROCKPOOL ZONES

Rockpools are divided into zones. The splash zone and the high-tide zone are rarely covered by the sea, so here you'll find just a few shore species, perhaps some seaweed, small crustaceans and common red beadlet anemones.

In the mid-tide zone, the part of the beach that is only left dry at low tide, the sealife becomes more interesting. Here among the barnacle-encrusted rocks and beds of mussels, you might discover interesting seaweed and sponges, brightly-coloured flat periwinkles, sea slugs, starfish and crabs.

The low-tide zone is accessible for only a few hours every few weeks, at unusually low tides. This is the perfect time to go rockpooling as you are most likely to make the best discoveries – seastars, brittle starfish, sea cucumbers, anemones, nudibranchs, sponges and kelps. Here you may also find hermit crabs, prawns and even fish.

HOW TO USE A SNORKEL AND FLIPPERS

THE undersea world is full of colour and marvel and with the simplest of equipment it is there for any fellow to admire. Just follow the correct use of a snorkel and flippers and you can enjoy a clear underwater view for hours on end.

1. Before you go into the water, ensure the mask fits your face. Without putting the strap on, hold the snorkel mask up to your face. Breathe in through your nose. The mask should seal perfectly and stay on, without you holding it, for as long as you breathe in. Now you can pass the strap over your head.

2. Position the small rubber strap that attaches the snorkel to your mask so that the snorkel passes just above your ear.

3. Put on your flippers. They should be snug, but not too tight.
4. Enter the water. Put the mouthpiece right into your mouth, biting down hard on it. Take a deep breath and submerge your head in the water, making sure the snorkel extends vertically above your head.
5. If the mask floods, raise your head, pull the lower edge away from your face and let the water drain out. A burst of air (try shouting the word 'two') should clear any water that may be in the snorkel shaft. Avoid any sudden movements as these can cause the snorkel to fill with water.
6. To dive below the surface of the water, inhale and hold your breath. To move around, keep your arms by your sides and, with your legs and ankles together, gently move your toes up and down. When ascending remember to clear the snorkel of water.

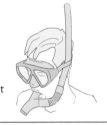

HOW TO PADDLE A KAYAK

KAYAKING is a fantastic way of exploring waterways and islands. At water level you'll have an excellent view of your aquatic surroundings and with the correct technique you'll find yourself fairly hurtling along.

1. The first technique to perfect is how to get into the kayak. Get your kayak floating in water deep enough to prevent it scraping on the bottom, but shallow enough for you to be able to put a foot down if necessary. Rest one blade of your paddle flat on the shore with the paddle shaft across your rear deck behind the cockpit. Now, grabbing both the shaft and cockpit in one hand, place one leg into the cockpit, slide your bottom over the seat and pull the other leg up and in. Straighten your legs, lean forward slightly and then bend at the knees so your feet are securely wedged in.

YOU WILL NEED

- Kayak
- Paddle
- Lifejacket or buoyancy aid

2. To grip the paddle, place your hands about shoulder-width apart, either side of the centre of the shaft, so that your elbows form slightly less than a 90-degree angle. The right hand should remain fixed, only rotating during strokes. The right wrist remains straight for a stroke on the right; it is rotated backwards for a stroke on the left. Only the paddle shaft rotates in the left hand. If you are using a left-handed paddle, you will need to reverse the process.

3. To go forward, every paddle stroke includes both a push with one arm and a pull with the other. With the bottom arm extended, but not straight, and the top hand around eye height with the elbow bent, place the blade in the water near your toes. Quickly dig with a spearing motion and pull the paddle blade back alongside the boat to approximately your hip. Lift the paddle blade and take a stroke on the other side. To turn the kayak, pull a wider arc on the opposite side to the direction in which you wish to turn.

4. To paddle in reverse, rotate your body so that the shoulder on the side of the stroke is right back. Place the paddle parallel to the boat with the blade flat on the water, back down. Push down with the bottom hand and raise the top hand to about eye height. This will set the blade at an angle of about 45 degrees. It should also be fully submerged. Keeping the blade close to the line of the boat and the shaft virtually vertical, pull the stroke through and repeat on the other side.

5. To stop the kayak, place the back of the blade in the water slightly behind your seat with your elbow in tight against your body and hold the paddle motionless as the kayak drags it through the water. The kayak will turn slightly to the stroke side. Repeat on the other side. It should be possible to come to a complete stop in two or three strokes.

HOW TO USE BINOCULARS

A NYONE who spends time outdoors should own a pair of binoculars. However, like every other indispensable tool, binoculars are practically useless unless correctly handled and adjusted. Here are some easy, step-by-step instructions to making the four adjustments necessary to get the best out of your binoculars.

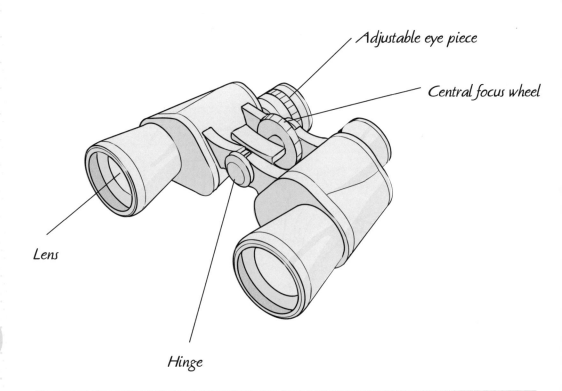

Adjustable eye piece

Central focus wheel

Lens

Hinge

HINGE

The two halves of the binoculars are joined together in the centre with a hinge. You can move the halves in and out (or up and down) until they are the right distance apart for your eyes. Look through the glasses and find something to focus on, such as a dark tree branch against the sky, a street sign or a person. You will probably see two images at the same time. Fold the glasses together along the hinge until you have one big, clear, circular field of vision. If you get dark patches or crescents in the centre or on the sides they are too close together.

CENTRAL FOCUS

Focus your view with both eyes open by turning the central focus wheel. Holding the binoculars in both hands, reach to the centre and turn the wheel in the middle until you have the sharpest, clearest view possible.

How to adjust the binoculars one eye at a time

You have focused the two sides of the binoculars at the same time. However, the vision in your two eyes is probably not identical. You need to adjust your binoculars so that each side is in focus for each eye. You do this by using the adjustable eyepiece, which is called the diopter.

The adjustable eyepiece is the one that turns and most binoculars have it on the right-hand side. It should have a simple scale on the underside that reads something like '– 0 +'. Set the adjustable eyepiece to 0 or the middle of the scale.

1. Close your right eye and look through the binoculars with just your left eye. Using the central focus, get the left eye's image as sharp as possible.

2. Then close your left eye and look through with your right eye. Ignoring the central focus, turn the adjustable eyepiece back and forth with your right hand until you get the sharpest image you can in your right eye.

3. With both eyes open, the object should now be in sharp focus. To check, use the central focus to focus on something else at a different distance. Then alternate looking at it with one eye at a time. The image should be in the same sharp focus with each eye.

4. When you have the adjustable eyepiece in the right position, look at the scale and remember that setting. This is your personal setting for that pair of binoculars. If you lend them to a friend you can make sure they are returned to this setting.

Having made these adjustments, each time you choose to look through your binoculars you need only adjust the central focus.

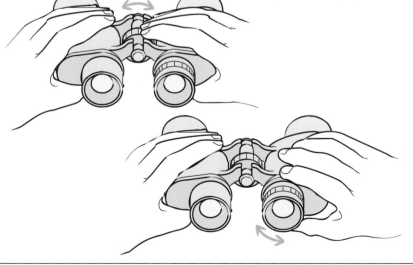

FUN AND GAMES

FINDING FOSSILS

FOSSILS are traces of the presence of eons-old plants and creatures and their activities, including root tunnels, burrows and footprints. Fossils come in a variety of sizes, from small insect impressions to large dinosaur bones. A fossil is like a time machine, capable of taking a chap back millions of years, and all that's required for this trip is some basic information, a suitable location and a good deal of patience.

YOU WILL NEED

- Toilet paper for wrapping your fossils
- Plastic food bags for protecting your fossils
- Old toothbrush for cleaning up your fossils
- Field journal for recording your finds
- Hammer, chisels and safety goggles (all optional)

WHERE TO LOOK FOR FOSSILS

It's worth researching the best places to look for fossils. The foreshore is often the most common place to look, but you can find a fossil almost anywhere. Keep your eyes open for unusual shapes and textures – objects that are clearly different from the rock around them.

Shingle beaches: fossils can be washed out of cliffs and from below beach level, and be caught between the shingle on the beach.

Under rocks: move stones or boulders and look under rocks, because you might discover an important find that's previously been hidden from view.

On the tide line: look for amber that has become tangled up in seaweed and try to spot the smaller fossils that may have been missed by other collectors.

On scree slopes: fossils can fall from cliffs on to scree slopes. Because the fossils are normally heavier than the scree, they tend to accumulate at the bottom of these slopes.

At a quarry: the types of fossils that can be found depends on what sort of material has been exposed by excavation at the bottom of a disused quarry. This can be a dangerous area, so please take every safety precaution necessary. Fossils may also be found on quarry or pit spoil heaps.

Along a riverbank: fossils can be washed up on riverbeds or out of the riverbank. Some rivers have cliff faces and beaches that are very similar to seaside locations.

In small streams: small shallow streams, particularly those with slow-moving currents, can yield some excellent finds. Fossils can travel for miles down these streams.

On a farm field: farms are often a good place to search for fossils as years of ploughing can lift fossils to the surface. This is especially true in chalky areas. It is very important to get the farmer's permission before you start digging.

WHEN YOU FIND A FOSSIL

If possible, take a photograph of the fossil before you attempt to dig it out. When extracting it, be as careful as possible, especially if you are using a hammer and chisel. Use an old toothbrush to clean around it as much as you can, then wrap it in toilet paper and place it in a plastic bag to keep it well protected. Remember to enclose details of exactly where it was found. As soon as you can, visit your local library to try and determine what it is. If you are still mystified, take the fossil to a local museum to see if they can identify it.

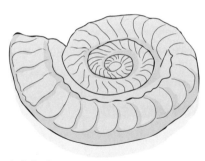

Shell fossil

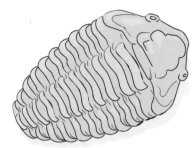

Ammonite fossil

Fern fossil

HOW TO SKIM STONES

THE simplest games are often the best. 'Skimming' a stone involves throwing it into the sea or a lake so that it bounces as many times as possible across the surface.

YOU WILL NEED

- Pebble beach or a number of small stones
- Large stretch of water

THE STONE

Your stone should be oval or triangular in shape and as smooth as possible. It needs to be about the size of the palm of your hand and should be heavy enough not to be blown off course by the wind, but light enough so that you can throw it accurately.

THE WATER

You will need a calm body of water large enough to take a strong throw. A reservoir, lake or estuary is preferable, but throwing from a beach into a calm sea can also produce good results.

Basic technique

1. Hold the stone comfortably with your thumb and pointer fingers around most of its edges. Face right if you're right-handed or left if you are left-handed, bringing your arm back.

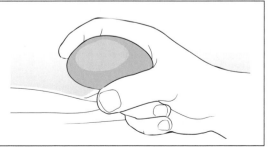

2. Bend your knees, anchor your back foot and step towards the water with your leading foot. Tilt your stone back about 10 or 20 degrees, or more if there are strong waves.

Advanced skimming

Once you're proficient at this technique, improve your skimming by throwing your stone at a very slight upward angle, but with greater force. It's tricky, but this should enable you to:

- Make the stone jump over other objects.
- Skim from high above the water.
- Skim standing a long way back.
- Make the stone fly a long way before its first skip.
- Throw with backwards spin.

3. Throw the stone. Let go of the stone at about knee height and aim for a spot 2–3 m (6–10 ft) out from the shore. Try to flick your wrist to give a slight horizontal spin to the pebble. To achieve maximum bounce, the stone should hit the water with plenty of downward force, but with its flat surface parallel to the water.

ROCK CLIMBING

CLIMBING rock faces or mountains is a serious business and should only be undertaken by those with the correct equipment and training. However, as any hiker or rockpool enthusiast will testify, an ability to scramble over a few rocks, without ropes and harnesses, can transform a pleasant afternoon into a real adventure.

PREPARATION

Keep your pack as light as possible, stash away anything you might usually hang on your rucksack and keep the bulk of the weight low down. Consider your route. Usually tracks are well worn and follow the line of least resistance along a natural feature, but take nothing for granted.

Trace the line and see how it looks higher up. Then think about your descent; climbing up is a jolly sight easier than climbing down. Remember, climbing can be dangerous, so you should always have a companion when rock-climbing.

THE REST STEP

On steep ascents, it is important to conserve your energy. Mountaineers use a rest step, which allows the climber to give his leg muscles a momentary rest on each step.

1. Step forward with your right leg, while keeping your weight on your back (left) leg and momentarily 'locking' the back leg in a straight position.

2. Swing your left leg forward to take the next step, while locking and transferring your weight to your right (now the back) leg.

3. Repeat the process with each step, always putting your weight on your locked rear leg.

ON THE CLIMB

- Keep your knees bent and your weight low, and to avoid fatigue, climb with your legs and your feet, using your arms and hands for stability only. Remember that the lower body powers and the upper body balances.
- Don't panic. If you find yourself in a bit of a tizz, take deep breaths, squeeze your handholds really hard, then deliberately relax them and focus on the climb.
- Your body is well-balanced when your back is straight and your weight is directed straight down on to your footholds.

PERFECTING YOUR TECHNIQUE

- Move one hand or foot at a time while the other three are on holds.
- Check each hold is secure by thumping or kicking it, before putting your weight on it.

GETTING DOWN

- Descending always feels less comfortable than ascending. If it's too steep to face outwards, you'll have to face inwards, but make sure you've got enough space to be able to look down.
- As with climbing up, move one hand or foot at a time and check each placement – you could have shifted it on the way up.
- If your pal is already below you, ask him to point out where the holds are. Move your hands down first and try to choose handholds at or below your waist to allow you to move down to lower footholds easily.
- Don't be tempted to jump until you are sure you can land safely.

HOW TO SKI

YOU WILL NEED

- Cold-weather clothing
- Pair of skis
- Pair of ski poles
- A gentle, snow-covered slope

IT'S all very well having fun in the snow, but if a guy is going to make real headway in the white stuff he's going to have to master the art of skiing.

SETTING OFF DOWNHILL

1. Begin by slowly 'walking' – sliding one ski ahead of the other – just to get your balance. Now find a gentle slope and stand with your shoulders and

hands facing downhill and your skis placed sideways. Taking small steps, point your skis downhill, bend your knees, but keep your weight on your poles.

2. When you're ready, release the weight from your poles and slide downhill, keeping your skis at hip distance apart for maximum stability. Remember to bend at the knees and ankles so your shins are close to the tongue of your boots. Look ahead and steer your skis gently with your feet to keep them parallel and pointing downhill. When not planting your poles, keep them tucked under your arms and facing behind you at all times.

SLOWING DOWN

1. Form a 'snowplough' with your skis – a V-shaped position with the tails of both skis apart and the tips together.

2. Gradually make the wedge wider as you ski straight down the hill until you come to a stop.

TURNING

1. If you want to turn, keep your body still, but apply slightly more pressure to your outside leg (the one on the opposite side to the direction in which you wish to turn).

2. Push your outside knee forwards and into the turn. Before you slow down so much that you stop, initiate a new turn by transferring pressure to the other ski and turn back.

HOW TO SKATE

YOU may think getting across the ice on a pair of boots with little more than a fishknife on the soles is going to be a tricky business, but stay relaxed, keep your head up and your back straight, and follow these simple tips – you'll be flying along in no time.

SKATING FORWARDS

1. When you get out on to the ice, first establish your balance. Keep your feet together with the toes turned slightly out. Hold your arms in front of you at hip level with the palms facing down, as if they are on an imaginary table.

2. Now position your feet so that they're parallel, about 20 cm (8 in) apart, bend your knees so that you can't see your toes and lean your shoulders forward so they are above your knees.

YOU WILL NEED

• Skates
• Frozen lake or river capable of taking your weight (see 'How Thick is the Ice', pages 88–89)

3. Keep your body loose and relaxed. If you're right-footed then put your weight on your left foot and push in a diagonal direction outwards, with your right foot behind and to the right of you.

4. Once the leg is fully extended, your weight should be shifted from the back leg to the front leg in preparation for the next stride. The back leg should now be brought back to its original position, alongside the glide leg. Now bring the right foot back so that it's next to the left and repeat the process.

HOW TO STOP

To stop, place one skate behind you with the toe facing away from you and gently drag it behind until you come to a halt.

SKATING BACKWARDS

To skate backwards, move your feet in half circles pushing backwards with your right foot and letting your left glide with it. Imagine you are squeezing yourself out of a tube of toothpaste. Repeat until you are gliding effortlessly backwards!

PUDDLE CURLING

WHEN the big freeze comes and there's little else to do but play, draw yourself out a curling rink. You don't need a massive sheet of ice, in fact even a puddle will do, but find yourself some suitable stones and get in training for the Winter Olympics!

YOU WILL NEED

- Curling stones
- Black, red and blue marker pens
- Frozen ground or large puddle
- Garden brush or cloth for 'sweeping'

THE STONES

Competition curling has two teams of four people, although of course you don't have to replicate this, but each player must have two stones. The stones should be flat-bottomed, as heavy as possible and of a size in proportion to the size of your rink.

THE RINK

Real curling is played on a sheet of ice 44.5 m (146 ft) long by 4.5 m (14 ft 9 in) wide. However, it's unlikely you'll find a sheet of ice this big, so just make sure that, using your black marker pen, you can mark out an area on your frozen ground or puddle that's about ten times as long as it is wide. Next, using the red pen to outline the centre circle, the blue pen for the middle circle and the black for the outer circle, draw a target (as illustrated across the page) – known as a 'house' – a step or two in from one end. Finally, at a similar distance from the other end, draw a straight line across the width of the ring; this is called the 'hack line'.

HOW TO PLAY

Each team takes turns delivering eight stones each (two per player) to the house, aiming to be the closest stone to the centre of the target. Players start the stone moving at the hack line. If you are playing on a small rink, place your pointer finger horizontally behind the stone and give it a sharp push. It is permissible, and a good tactic, to shunt other stones into or out of position. After all the stones have been delivered, the 'end' is complete.

CLEAN SWEEPING

As in real curling, you can sweep in front of the stone to make it go further. Try using a garden brush or, if you're playing in a puddle, a cloth to shine the surface. Take care not to touch the stone, though, or it will be deemed out of play.

THE SHOTS

The draw: when a stone stops in the scoring area.
The guard: when a stone stops in front of a stone in scoring position.
The takeout: when a stone physically knocks an opposing team's stone from its position.
The hammer: the definitive final shot.

THE SCORING

During each end, only one team can score. The team with the stone closest to the centre of the house scores one point and one additional point for every stone nearer the centre than the nearest opponent's stone. Some of the possible scorings are illustrated here with the light green team's score given first. A match consists of 10 ends. If the result is tied, additional ends are played until a winner emerges.

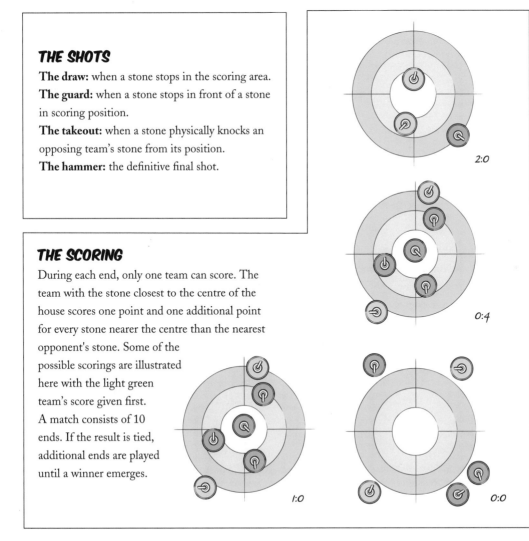

2:0

0:4

1:0

0:0

SNOW AND ICE SCULPTURE

WE all recall the childhood thrill of making a snowman at the first flurry of snow, but few of us continue this 'art' into adulthood. Yet, with a good supply of snow or ice, there is little to stop us creating a stunning seasonal masterpiece!

1. Sketch out the front view of your design on paper and draw a grid pattern over it. Copy the grid and draw, as precisely as possible, the rear view of the design.

2. Using shovels of heavily-beaten snow, build a solid snow block on a rough base so it is elevated above the ground. Once the block is of a satisfactory height, mark out a similar grid, with the end of a trowel.

YOU WILL NEED

- Block of ice or a recent downfall of snow
- Shovel
- Pointed stick or chisel
- Gardening tools such as hand trowels, small axes, hoes and bulb-planting scoops for carving, snow removal and texturing

3. Referring to your diagram, sketch the front outline of the design in the block with a pointed stick or chisel. Repeat the task for the rear of the sculpture. (We've shown the rear design on the side of the block here).

TIPS

• *Snow sculptures will last for days if the temperature stays below freezing, but only a day or so if it gets warmer*

• *At night, spray your finished snow sculpture with a gentle mist of water to hold it together for a little while longer.*

61

4. From the rear, begin by roughly removing the 'negative space' around your design with a hand axe. When you're about three-quarters of the way through the block, swap to clear away the front side. Having revealed your outline, begin to mould the features of your statue with smaller tools and your hands. If you make a mistake at any time just plaster the snow back firmly into place and have another go.

SAILING A DINGHY

CUTTING through the open water in a sailing dinghy is one of life's great pleasures, but the capable sailor has to master both the techniques and the science of sailing.

YOU WILL NEED

- Sailing dinghy
- Lake or estuary
- Lifejacket or buoyancy aid

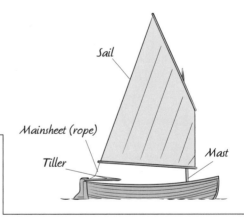

Sail

Mainsheet (rope)

Mast

Tiller

IN THE DINGHY

Sit on the boat with your back to the wind, just in front of the tiller. Move your weight towards the edge of the boat if it begins to tip or keel over with the wind in the sails. Use one hand to grip the rope (mainsheet) holding the sail; place the other hand on the tiller. Direct the boat by pushing the tiller in the opposite direction to the direction in which you want to turn. Keep the movement of the tiller to a minimum to prevent oversteering.

Pay attention to how the sail is reacting to the wind. When the front of the sail, just behind the mast, flutters in the breeze, you lose power. To start moving, pull the sail in a little, so the wind fills the sail and it pulls taut. Adjust the position whenever the wind changes direction or you need to change course.

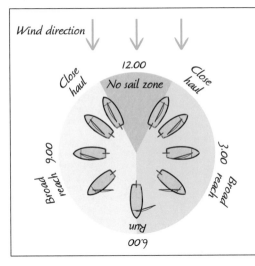

Close haul

12.00

No sail zone

Close haul

9.00

Broad reach

3.00 Broad reach

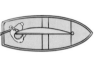

Run

6.00

POINTS OF SAIL

If your dinghy is pointing in any direction in the 'sail zone', you'll find the boat moves along. Your speed, however, depends upon the angle between the wind and the sail. To go upwind or across the wind, a boat must get lift from its sails. Sails develop the most lift at an angle of about 30 degrees to the wind blowing across the boat. To get the most force out of a sail when on a close haul, pull the sail in until it just stops flapping. On a broad reach or run, let out the sail as far as it will go.

Wind direction

63

TACKING

As you enter the 'no-sail zone' your sail will start flapping and you'll find yourself coming to a halt. It is impossible to sail directly into the wind. Instead, you have to take a zigzag route, sailing (tacking) from 1.30 to 10.30 on the points of sail diagram and back again.
To tack: with the boat moving forward, push the tiller away from you slowly. As the boom swings across, duck under it and move

to the other side of the boat, switching tiller and mainsheet hands. Now begin to pull the tiller back to a central position. Pull the mainsheet in until the sail stops flapping. The dinghy should still be moving forward, but on a diagonal line to the point you want to reach. By continuing to tack back and forth, either when you get too near land or you lose the wind, you will make headway against the wind.

JIBING

Your boat will be travelling fastest when the wind is behind you, but not directly behind (at 6.00). To progress swiftly you will need to perform a similar manoeuvre to tacking, this time changing your course between 4.30 and 7.30.

To start jibing, pull the tiller towards you and manually pull the sail across to the middle. As the wind fills the sail from the opposite side and swings across the boat, move across yourself and ease the sail out quickly. You should speed ahead, but prepare to reverse the procedure when you cross the line of the wind at 6.00 once again.

HOW TO SURF

THE exhilarating feeling of riding a wave is one that will appeal to any sporting fellow. With a little practice and application, it really isn't that difficult to get yourself coasting into the shore. However, take a little care, remember the sea can be a fickle mistress!

YOU WILL NEED

- Surfboard
- Beach with breaking waves
- Wetsuit (in cold waters)

1. Hold the board upright at arm's length with a hand on each side. Walk out to where the waves are breaking, then turn and place your board flat at your side with the nose facing towards the beach. Keeping an eye on the waves that are coming in behind you, lie down in the middle of the board, putting your chin on the mark that tells you you're in the middle.

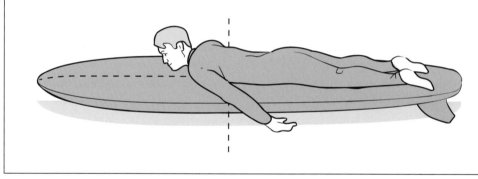

2. You're aiming to catch the wave in the moment before it breaks into white water. When you spot a likely wave, paddle with both arms as it starts to pick you up. Make sure that you're starting to paddle along the wave and not just straight into shore. Lie on your chest, your head up, looking ahead. Arch your neck and back to aim the board's nose upwards. You should feel the board rise in the water as the wave picks you up and your speed in the water increases.

3. Wait a second or stroke once, then put your hands on the board beside your shoulders, palms down as if you were going to do a push-up

Propel your upper body upwards and at the same time sweep your feet under you. Make sure your feet are lying on the line down the middle of the board. When you come up, remember to keep low. If you stand erect you will fall.

4. Face sideways, one hip towards the nose, the other towards the tail. Your feet should be shoulder-width apart, but centred on the board, and you'll need to bend your knees and crouch slightly to keep your balance. Hold your arms slightly higher than your waist so that you can just see them.

5. Lean forwards or backwards, or even step forwards or backwards, to make the board plane evenly along the water.

BUILDING A MEGA-SANDCASTLE

ONCE they've relaxed and topped up their tans, most adventurous types will feel the need for some activity, and on a beach, with all the materials to hand, what better way to pass an hour or two than by building a mega-sandcastle that will be the envy of your fellow holiday-makers. Your castle can be as elaborate or as simple as you like, but remember that sooner or later all your efforts will be swept away by the tide, and we don't want any tears!

Before you start have an idea in your head, or make a sketch, of how you want your sandcastle to look. Most structures are a combination of towers and connecting walls, but by varying the size of your towers, introducing geometric patterned walls and incorporating arches, turrets and ramparts, you can make sure your castle is really impressive!

YOU WILL NEED

- Sandy beach
- Bucket and spade
- Smaller tools, such as knives and trowels (these are all optional)

1. Find a level, sandy area near the water, but not so close that the incoming tide sweeps away your work before it's finished. Dig down to where the sand is dark and moist, and scoop wet sand into a central pile. Make sure your sand is of a smooth consistency, adding water if necessary, and gradually create a large foundation platform about 50 cm (20 in) high, packing the sand in tightly.

2. Now build the towers. Flatten wet sand into pancakes by jiggling – gently shaking from side to side – one or two handfuls. Allow the sand to settle and try not to pound or pack it so much that you squeeze the water out. Place larger patties on the bottom and gently shake the patties from side to side as you pile them, so that the sand settles. Use smaller handfuls as the tower gets higher, so that it tapers at the top and won't fall over before you get to carve it. Finally, seal your towers by gently pouring water over them.

3. To connect the walls, scoop as much wet sand as you can hold in two hands and jiggle it into a brick shape about 10 x 5 cm (4 x 2 in). Keep your bricks the same shape and size and lay them along the length of the wall. Put another layer on top, overlapping the lower bricks, and continue adding layers until you reach the required height.

4. Carve the towers and the walls into shapes using tools such as a small trowel, a putty knife or plastic utensils. Create arches by gently tunnelling your way through a wall. Begin at the base, then enlarge and shape the opening by taking off thin layers of sand. To build staircases, make a gently sloping ramp and carve the steps with a knife. Finally, dig a moat around the castle – it might help it survive for a few more minutes!

HOW TO PLAY DODGEBALL

W HEN half a dozen fit and able lads want to expend a little surplus energy, there's nothing better than an outdoor version of the game played in school gymnasiums across the world.

YOU WILL NEED

- Equal number of players
- Up to three footballs, volleyballs or similar-sized soft balls
- Patch of land about the size of a tennis or basketball court

BEFORE YOU START

Pick your teams. Try to make the game as fair as possible, so don't put all the athletes and sportsmen on the same team! You'll need at least three-a-side for a decent game and if there are more than six-a-side, use the extra men as reserves. You'll find you get exhausted pretty quickly.

CHOOSE YOUR PLAYING AREA

The ideal size is about 20 x 10 m (65 x 33 ft), but don't worry too much – just make sure everyone knows where the boundaries are. Try to choose a surface without too many obstacles to trip over or run into, but a tree somewhere on the field can provide an interesting variation on the game.

THE OBJECT OF THE GAME

What you need to do is eliminate all the opposing players by getting them 'out'. As you would expect, when a team lose their last player, they have been defeated. You can get a player out by:
- Hitting an opposing player below the shoulders with a thrown ball.
- Catching a ball thrown by your opponent before it touches the ground.

THE OPENING RUSH

To begin the game, place the ball or balls in the centre of the pitch. Teams then take a position at each end. Following a signal by a neutral party, the team race to retrieve the balls.

TIPS

• Before the game begins gather your team and choose a "hit list." of the top three best players on your opponents' team. Assign each of them a number and during the game call out the number for anyone with a ball to pursue them at the same time.

• As soon as one of your opponents is hit, aim for another one. There's often a split second where people are stunned when one of their teammates get hit

• Whenever possible, hide your ball behind your back. Get the whole team to put their hands behind their backs to confuse your opponents.

• Don't look at the person you are throwing at; try pointing at one player casually and then throw at a different one.

• Aim at the shins. Aiming at feet can make the ball bounce on the foot and aiming for the knees runs the risk of the opponent catching it.

VARIATIONS ON THE DODGEBALL THEME

Killerball: one or two players become the 'taggers' and, using the ball, they have to tag the other players by hitting them below the knee with the ball. Players who are tagged change places with the tagger and become the tagger instead.

Pin-dodge: each team has four sticks or tins at their end of the court. If a team's 'pin' gets knocked over, either by accident or by a ball thrown by the other team, all players on the other team return to play. Once knocked over, a pin must stay down. The game ends when all a team's players are eliminated or when all a team's pins are knocked over.

Dr Dodgeball: each team has an assigned 'doctor'. When players are hit, they fall on the ground and wait for the doctor to come and save them. Once he has tagged them, they can get up and play again. If Dr Dodgeball is hit, he is out and his healing powers are lost.

Prisonball: when a player is hit, he gets put in 'prison' behind the opposing team. To get out of prison, he must hit one of the opposing team with the ball from behind.

CAPTURE THE FLAG

THIS traditional scouting game has been around for years, but is still marvellous fun to play on a hot and sunny day. You need hardly any equipment – just some enthusiastic pals and a sense of adventure.

PREPARATION

Since a big part of this game involves hiding and sneaking around corners, choose an area with interesting hiding places, obstacles and so on, and a boundary line such as a brook or trail. Agree on the time-limit for your game and then pick two equally numbered teams and send them to opposite ends of the area. Each team must also choose a landmark – a tree or rock – for their 'prison'.

YOU WILL NEED

- Playing area the size of a football pitch
- At least ten people (you will need an even number)
- Two flags

PLANTING THE FLAG

Each team has three minutes to plant a flag in their area. The flag must be head height and visible, although it is permissible to place it as inconspicuously as possible.

START THE GAME

After the signal is given for the start of game, the objective for each team is to enter the enemy's territory, capture the flag and carry it across the line into home territory without being caught. Players may be posted to guard the flag, but they can't get closer than 10 m (33 ft) to it. If an enemy player goes into the 10 m (33 ft) circle, they may then follow him.

OTHER VERSIONS OF THE GAME

Checkpoint Charlie: instead of a jail, take prisoners to a 'Checkpoint Charlie' at the centreline, where they can be exchanged and freed.

Hidden flag: each team hides their flag out of sight. Before starting the game one player from each team is shown the position of the enemy flag.

Get out of jail free: all team members caught in the jail can be set free when a single team-mate touches the jail, but they do not have free passage back to their territory.

Jailbreak!: as soon as all jailed members of a team see that their flag has been captured, they are instantly freed to help defend their homeland.

Night-time capture the flag: two lanterns are used to mark the centre line, while two others mark where the flags are.

GO TO JAIL

Any player found in the enemy's territory may be captured by grasping him long enough for the captor to say 'Caught!' three times. When a player is captured he must go with his captor to the prison. A prisoner may be released by a team-mate touching him, provided the prisoner at that time is touching the prison with a hand or a foot. The prisoner can then return safely to their own territory. The person freeing the player is immediately back in the game, but he himself may still be tagged and put in jail. A rescuer can rescue only one prisoner at a time.

VICTORY

If the flag is successfully captured, it must be carried across the line into home territory. If the raider is caught before he reaches home, the flag is set up again at the point where it was rescued and the game continues as before. If neither side captures the enemy's flag within the agreed time, the game is won by the team with the most prisoners.

TIPS

• Divide your team into border guards, scouts (to find the flag), stealers (to get the flag) and rangers (to get people out of jail, chase anyone who gets past the border guards and replace captured players).

• When selecting people for a job, think about what their strengths are. Scouts should be nippy and perceptive, stealers need to be your fastest players and guards should be the strongest.

• Remember to communicate with team-mates – you can do this with codes or just by shouting.

THROWING AND CATCHING A BOOMERANG

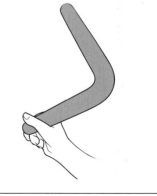

I T'S an exhilarating moment. You've taken a piece of carved wood, thrown it over 30 m (30 yd) away, turned and found it flying back into your hand. But it's not quite as easy as that. Accurately throwing a boomerang requires attention to technique and a fair degree of patience and practice.

THE GRIP

Hold the boomerang with the curved side towards your body and the flat side facing away from you. The 'elbow' of the boomerang can be facing either forwards or backwards. Pinch the boomerang lightly between your thumb and forefinger, allowing friction to keep the boomerang in your hand during the throw.

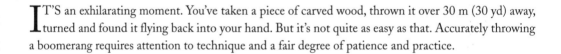

YOU WILL NEED

• Boomerang
• Open field at least half the size of a football pitch
• Warm day with a gentle breeze

THE THROW

Always throw your boomerang overarm style, in the same way that you would throw a baseball or a cricket ball. Aim at the horizon, around 10 m (33 ft) above the ground (often you can aim at the tops of the trees surrounding your field). Now cock back your boomerang and prepare to throw. Release the boomerang at the top of your throw, snap your wrist and allow it to force its way out of your hand. Thrown correctly, the boomerang will fly in a circle and reach the apex of its flight at the point furthest away from you.

THE LAUNCH ANGLE

The amount of tilt you impart to the boomerang has a crucial impact on the quality of the flight. In calm to light wind conditions, tilt the boomerang 20–30 degrees away from the vertical. This should give it a higher, more rounded flight. In higher winds, stand the boomerang up towards the vertical, to make it fly closer to the ground.

THE CATCH

If your throw was a good one, you should be able to follow the boomerang's trajectory and get ready to catch it. Once the boomerang is slowly winging its way towards you and is below shoulder height, prepare to trap it between the palms of your hands. Place one hand above and one below your boomerang and 'clap' your hands together. Aim for the middle part of the boomerang and try to avoid the faster-moving wing-tips. If you lose sight of the boomerang during its flight, assume the 'lost boomerang position': turn your back on where you think it will come from, crouch down, cover your head with your hands – and cross your fingers!

IF YOUR BOOMERANG DOESNT COME BACK...

• If it returns, but lands in front of you, turn and throw slightly more into the wind.

• If it returns, but lands behind you, turn and throw slightly more away from the wind.

• If it returns, but is too high to catch, try a softer throw or alter the launch angle (see above).

• If it hits the ground before it reaches you, throw harder or alter the launch angle (see above).

• If it flies straight to the ground, check your grip and throwing technique.

MAKING A KITE

I T'S always a blast flying a kite on a blustery day, but if you've made your own kite it can be even more fun. Here's an easy-to-assemble kite you can make while at camp.

YOU WILL NEED

- Two strong, straight wooden bamboo canes or dowelling rods, 90 cm (36 in) and 102 cm (40 in) long
- String
- Knife to make notches
- Scissors
- Sheet of strong paper or cut-open bin-liner, 102 cm (40 in) square
- Pens or paints
- Sticky tape or glue
- Ribbons

1. Carve a notch deep enough to hold the string in each end of the canes. Place the shorter one across the centre of the longer one to form a cross. At the crosspoint, tie the canes together with the string.

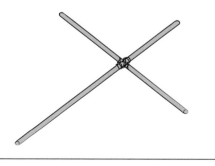

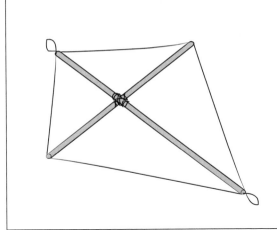

2. Cut a piece of string long enough to create a frame for the kite. Make a loop in the top notch and fasten it by wrapping the string around the cane. Stretch the string around the four points of the crossed canes, making a similar loop at the bottom. Secure by wrapping the string a few times around the top of the cane and cutting off what you don't need. This string shouldn't be slack, but it shouldn't be so tight that it bends the frame either.

3. Lie the paper or bin-liner flat and place the cane-and-string frame facedown on top. Cut around the frame, leaving about 2–3 cm (¾–1¼ in) around the edges and fold these over, taping or glueing them around the frame, so that the material is taut. Decorate your kite, using bright colours to ensure it can be easily identified in the air.

4. Cut a piece of string about 120 cm (48 in) long and fix it to the loops at the top and bottom of the kite. Create another small loop in this string just above the intersection of the two canes. Attach your flying line to this loop.

5. Make a tail by tying a piece of ribbon every 10 cm (4 in) along a short length of string and attach it to the loop at the bottom of the kite.

6. When you're finished, hold your kite up by the string to see if it's balanced. If it doesn't hang evenly, balance it by sticking additional paper to one side.

BEACH-TOWEL VOLLEYBALL

THIS variation on beach volleyball is great fun when a few pals are hanging out together on the beach. You'll find you soon become pretty adept at sending and catching the balloons – and some unlucky chap might well end up getting a bit of a soaking.

YOU WILL NEED

- Four or more people (you need an even number)
- Beach or open area
- Rope or volleyball net
- One towel for every two people
- Balloons filled with water

TIPS

- If you'd like to be a little more competitive, try using a beach ball instead of a balloon

- Remember, communication is the key. Keep talking and make sure you are all heading in the same direction

PLAYING THE GAME

A water-filled balloon is placed on the towel of one of the pairs.
The pair must then work together to flick their towel, propelling the
balloon into the air, across the net to the other team. One of the pairs
on the other team must then try to catch the balloon with their towel
and return it the same way.

SETTING UP

Set up a volleyball net or lie a rope down to mark the
centre of the court. Divide into two teams of equal
sporting prowess and direct each team to stand on
either side of the net. Each pair should have one large
beach towel and each person should grab two corners of
the towel, so that it is spread between the pair.

WINNING THE GAME

It's up to you! You can keep
points, try to get as many as
possible of the volleys back and
forth without dropping the
balloon or just see who ends up
the wettest!

WILDERNESS SURVIVAL

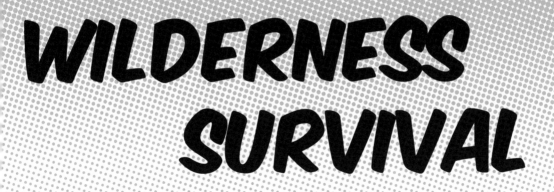

ASSEMBLING A SURVIVAL KIT

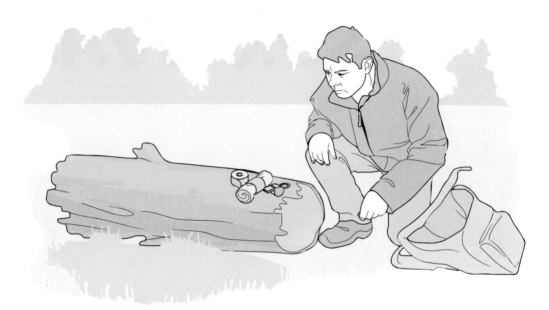

WE adventurers never like to think the worst, but even the best of us can end up in sticky situations. Whether you're preparing to go sailing, hiking or camping, it's worth preparing yourself for any emergency – a storm, injuries, getting stranded or losing your way.

Putting together your survival kit will depend upon the kind of adventure on which you are embarking, but the following points are worthy of consideration.

- Don't overpack. Being mobile is an important aspect of any expedition. Take what you can't do without and no more. Keep all the items together in a bag or a container, such as a large coffee tin.

- Consider your personal requirements and the particular environment you will be facing. Are there medicines you might need to take for allergies or existing medical conditions? Could a lack of drinking water be an issue?

- Make sure you take sufficient resources to enable you to spend at least one night outdoors. If you survive the first six hours of an emergency, your chances of holding out improve considerably.

Here are some of the things to consider when you make your own survival kit:

Navigation and signalling:
- Flares, orange surveyor's tape or bright coloured bandanna
- Whistle
- Compass
- Signal mirror

Food and drink:
- Water purification kit
- Fishing kit (line, hooks, weights)
- Pack of instant soup
- Heavy-duty aluminium foil
- Plastic bag

Tools:
- Flint
- Small multi-function (Swiss Army) knife
- Black shoe polish (useful as fuel for fire, animal repellent, marking and camouflage)
- Cable saw
- Dental floss (useful as thread, for fishing or lashing branches)
- Sewing kit

Miscellaneous:
- Black bin-liner
- Matches and candle
- Small first-aid kit comprising sterile dressing, antiseptic wipes, antiseptic cream, adhesive dressing strip, bandage, safety pins, small scissors, plasters (Band-Aids®)
- Pencil and notepad
- Toilet paper

FIND YOUR WAY WITH A MAP AND COMPASS

MOST afternoon hikers think they know how to use a map and a compass, but put these chaps in unfamiliar terrain and many would soon find themselves in a real pickle. The true adventurer, however, is practised in using these essential tools together to find his bearings and his way.

YOU WILL NEED

- Baseplate compass
- Map of relevant area
- Pencil

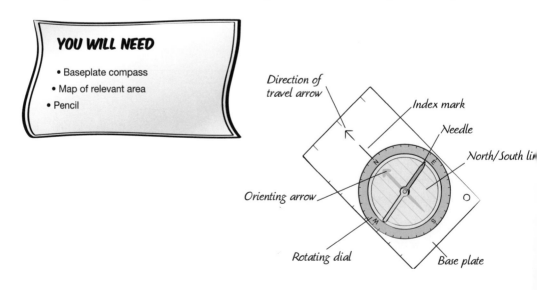

Direction of travel arrow

Index mark

Needle

North/South li...

Orienting arrow

Rotating dial

Base plate

1. The first thing you need to do is to identify your position on the map. Look around and pick a specific feature, natural or man-made – perhaps a church, a peak, bridge or road junction – that you can clearly identify on your map. Try to select a nearby landmark for the most accurate reading. Point the direction of travel arrow of the compass at the landmark and turn the dial until the orienting arrow on the dial is aligned with the red part of the needle. Find the index line, read your bearing and note it down.

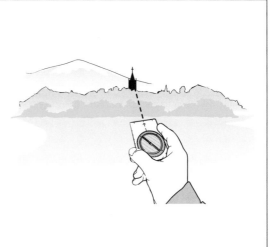

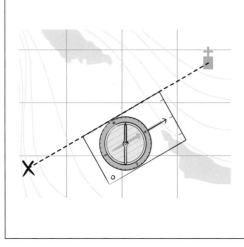

2. To find your location on the map, rotate the compass dial so that the bearing of your landmark is aligned with the direction of travel. Place the compass on the map and rotate it until the orienting arrow points north on the map. Then slide the compass around until the long edge goes through the landmark and draw a line along this edge. Your location is somewhere along this line. If it's not obvious exactly where you are, repeat the process with another landmark. This time, note where the lines intersect with each other. This is your position.

3. Now you've marked where you are, find the spot where you are heading on the map. Place the compass on the map so that the long edge connects the two positions, with the direction arrows pointing from the starting point to the place of destination.

Holding the compass firmly on the map in order to keep the baseplate steady, rotate the capsule until its north-south lines run parallel with the grid lines on the map and the orienting arrow points to the same direction as north on the map.

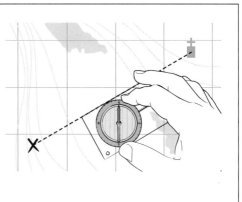

4. Now take the compass in your hand with the base held horizontally and the orienting arrow pointing straight ahead. Keep turning your body until the orienting arrow lines up with the red end of the needle. The direction of travel arrow now indicates the direction you should take. Remember to keep referring to your compass to ensure you are travelling in the right direction.

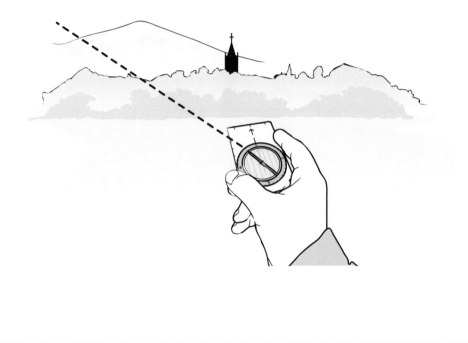

MAGNETIC DECLINATION

If your journey is any more than a short ramble you will need to compensate for magnetic declination – the difference between magnetic north as indicated on a compass and true north as used on a map. To do this, instead of rotating the compass housing until the orienting arrow is pointing along the grid lines, rotate it until the orienting arrow is aligned with the magnetic north lines as indicated in the diagram at the foot of the map.

CROSSING A RIVER

ENCOUNTERING a river or stream on a journey can present serious problems for the hiker. Getting across can be a little trickier than rolling up your trouser legs and paddling...

Caution: river crossings can be dangerous. If you are in any doubt as to whether you can cross the river safely, you should not attempt it.

CAN YOU CROSS THE RIVER?

Climb to a high vantage point and have a good look at the river. Then examine it at close hand. Assess how easy or difficult the crossing might be.

- Look for obstacles in the river – dead trees or submerged, sharp or slippery rocks.
- What is the riverbed like? Could there be soft sand or jagged stones?
- Will it be possible to get on land at the other side?
- How deep is the river and how fast-flowing? Don't attempt to cross if it is deeper than chest-height, or if it is very fast-flowing.

PREPARING TO CROSS

- Remove your trousers and shirt, but keep your footgear on to protect your feet and ankles from rocks and give you a firmer footing.
- Keep everything in one bundle. If you have to let go, it's easier to find one large pack than several small items.
- Waterproof your pack – or its contents – by wrapping it in a sturdy plastic liner.
- Undo the waist and chest straps of your pack. If you fall over, you'll want to throw it off quickly.
- Select a point on the opposite bank where you will exit the water.

CROSSING ALONE

- Find a strong pole about 7.5 cm (3 in) in diameter and 2 m (6 ft 6 in) long. Plant it firmly on your upstream side to break the current.
- Cross the stream so that you move through the downstream current at a 45-degree angle. Plant your feet firmly with each step and move the pole forwards, a little downstream from its previous position, but still upstream from you.
- With your next step, place your foot below the pole. Keep the pole well slanted so that the force of the current holds the pole against your shoulder.

IF YOU ARE CARRIED DOWNSTREAM

- Lie on your back with your feet pointing downstream.
- To steer away from oncoming obstacles, sit up and paddle with your hands to change direction.
- Keep your feet up to avoid them getting caught by rocks.

CROSSING IN A GROUP

It may be safer to cross the river in a group of three or four people. This technique enables each person to support the other members of the group.

- Face inwards with your heads close together, feet apart and arms firmly linked.
- The downstream person (the heaviest of the group) should face upstream.
- Only one person should move at a time, the two stationary people supporting the one moving.

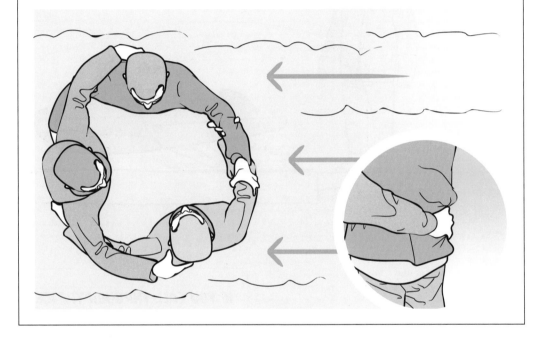

MAKESHIFT RAFT

In an emergency you can create your own flotation device by roping two logs together about 60 cm (2 ft) apart.

HOW THICK IS THE ICE?

10 cm (4 in)

15 cm (6 in)

'Thick and blue, tried and true.
Thin and crispy, way too risky.'

There is great fun to be had on the ice – skating, fishing and sledging – but you need to know when it's likely to be dangerous. Even if the weather has been below freezing for several days, never try to guess the thickness of the ice, because you could put your life in peril.

It takes steady, cold temperatures to form safe ice, and small ponds and lakes generally freeze more quickly than larger bodies of water. Once the water is frozen to a minimum thickness of 7.5–10 cm (3–4 in), it should be safe for travel by foot. New ice is fairly tough and elastic. Even if it cracks in all directions, it can support an average-sized person.

IF YOU FALL THROUGH THE ICE

- Don't panic.
- Turn towards the direction you came from.
- Place your hands and arms on the unbroken surface of the ice.
- Work forward on the ice by kicking your feet.
- If the ice breaks, maintain your position and slide forward again.
- Once you are lying on the ice, don't stand up. Roll away from the hole and spread your weight out until you are on solid ice.

20 cm (8 in)

30 cm (12 in)

WHAT TO LOOK FOR

- Look for bluish ice that is at least 10 cm (4 in) thick.
- Make test holes to check the thickness – beginning at the shore and continuing as you go further out.
- If the ice at the shoreline is cracked or squishy, stay off it.
- Don't go on the ice during thaws.
- Avoid 'honeycomb ice', where the ice turns black and loses its elasticity.
- Beware of snow. It acts as an insulator and slows down ice formation.
- Dark snow and dark ice are other signs of weak spots.
- Choose small bodies of water. Rivers and lakes are prone to wind and wave action, which can break ice up quickly.
- Avoid areas with piers, bridges and vegetation, which reduce both the thickness of the ice and its strength.

FACING UP TO A CHARGING BULL

A PLEASANT afternoon's stroll can turn into quite a hairy situation if you should accidentally stray into a field with a bull. However, if you don't alarm them, these creatures have no beef with you. Do check it really is a bull – look for udders, as many cows have horns too!

BULL FIELD CONDUCT

A bull will usually leave you alone unless you disturb him, so don't run, but walk calmly and confidently. Don't alarm him with screams, quick movements or loud noises either and look around for a safe haven, such as a fence, house or high ground.

THE RED HERRING

The idea that a bull is enraged by the colour red is a complete myth. Bulls are colour-blind and cannot distinguish between red and any other colour.

THE STAND-OFF

Before a bull charges he will perform a broadside stance by standing or walking sideways to you. He is now threatening you, so you should back away slowly, but don't run or turn your back to the bull

Alternatively, you can respond with the human version of a broadside threat, by stretching both your arms straight out in front of you, at right angles to your body, with your palms facing the bull. Sometimes this will force him to back off.

THE DISTRACTION MANOEUVRE

If the bull still shows signs of challenging you, slowly take hold of a hat, bag or a piece of clothing. As the bull charges, toss the object as hard as you can to the side. Bulls instinctively charge toward movement and he should follow the target and thus head away from you. Jump out of the way if you have to and put as much distance between you and the animal as you can. Hopefully he will now lose interest in you.

HOW TO AVOID BEING STRUCK BY LIGHTNING

THE way lightning illuminates the sky is beautiful and breathtaking from a safe vantage point, but it's a totally different prospect when you're caught in the middle of a storm. While nowhere is completely safe from lightning, a little knowledge and some common sense could help save your life.

HOW FAR AWAY IS THE LIGHTNING?

Folklore insists that, 'If you hear it, fear it. If you see it, flee it.' It's true that if you hear thunder, the lightning is close enough to worry about. Thunder arises from the collapse of the air around a bolt of lightning, so the two actually occur simultaneously. However, because light travels faster than sound, we see the lightning before we hear the thunder. When you see lightning, time the gap until you hear the thunder. If the time-delay between seeing the flash and hearing the thunder is less than 30 seconds, seek a safe location immediately. Every 10 seconds of time delay is equivalent to a distance of two miles between you and the storm, and lightning strikes have been calculated to be an average of two to three miles apart.

WHERE TO SHELTER DURING A LIGHTNING STORM

- Large enclosed buildings are safer than small or open structures, but stay away from windows and electrical appliances.
- Cars, trucks, buses and vans provide good shelter from lightning, but avoid contact with metal or conducting surfaces outside or inside the vehicle.

AREAS TO AVOID DURING A LIGHTNING STORM

- High places, open fields and ridges.
- Isolated trees and rain or picnic shelters, as well as shallow depressions in the earth.
- Flagpoles, telephone poles, electricity pylons and metal fences.
- Bodies of water, such as oceans, lakes, rivers and swimming pools.

THE LIGHTNING CROUCH

If you have no alternative or are taken unawares by a storm, do not lie down. Instead, get yourself down as low as you can, with as little of your body as possible touching the ground. This position is known as the 'lightning crouch'. Put your weight on your toes with the balls of your feet in the air and your heels tight together. You may also wish to put your hands over your ears to protect them from the thunder.

HITCHES AND LASHINGS – SOME USEFUL KNOTS

A CHAP won't find himself long in the field without having recourse to a knot. Learn a few of them – they're not difficult – and you'll soon discover these fascinating fellows are your best friends for building, fishing, mending and a hundred other purposes.

TWO HALF-HITCHES

This hitch is used to secure the end of a rope to a fixed object such as a post and is ideal for attaching a mooring line to a dock post or ring. You can tie and untie the knot while the load is attached and when it is tied around a post it is unlikely to slip down. It's simple to tie – just make sure that each half-hitch turns in the same direction.

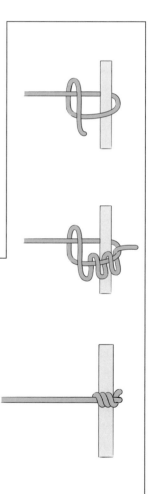

TIMBER HITCH

This knot is ideal for attaching a rope to a log, because it comes undone easily when not under strain, but is tight when tensed. When first learning this knot pay careful attention, though, as it's easy to make a mistake with the loop and the twists. Use at least three twists and add more if the object is large or heavy.

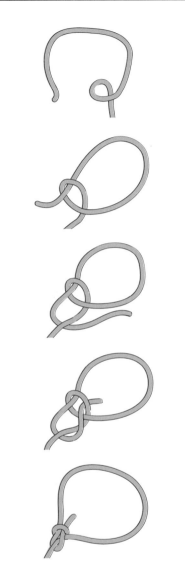

BOWLINE

Also called the 'yachtsman's friend' or the 'king of knots', this is one of the simplest ways of putting a fixed loop – that won't tighten – in the end of a rope. It is easy to tie and untie, it never slips or jams and has a high breaking strength.

THE TAUTLINE HITCH

This is an adjustable knot that is commonly used for tensioning guy lines on a tent. The knot can slide along the standing part, allowing you to remove the slack, but when placed under a load, it locks in place.

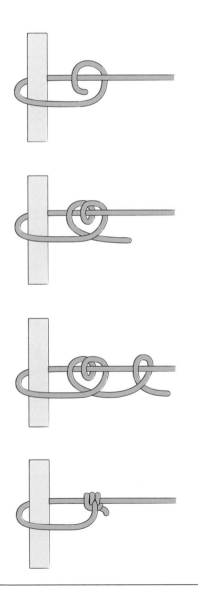

TRUCKER'S HITCH

This knot is marvellous for tying loads – such as a canoe to a car roof, binding a rolled sleeping bag or any application where a very tight rope is needed – even tightening the camp clothes-line. The added bonus is that the knot is easy to untie.

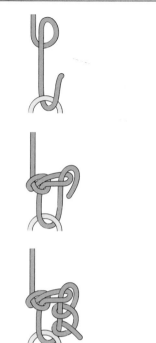

BARREL SLING

This knot, which isn't really a knot, enables you to hoist a bucket or suspend a pot to collect water. It can also be used for cooking and boiling, but use wire to hold the pot, because rope will burn in seconds.

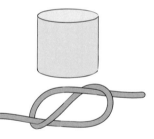

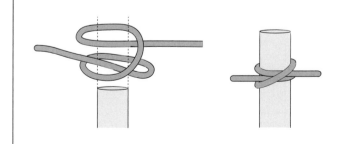

CLOVE HITCH

This basic knot can be used for securing a line to a fixed object, but it's most commonly employed to start and finish lashings.

SQUARE LASHING

When you are able to securely join two pieces of
wood together at right angles, you can construct
shelters, tables and other outside furniture. Begin
and fasten the lashing with a clove hitch.

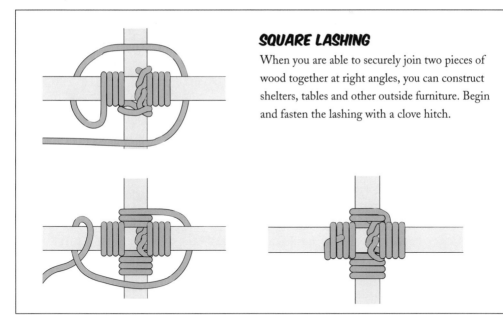

TRIPOD LASHING

Tripods are super outdoor structures,
invaluable for suspending cooking
pots over a fire, making shelters,
hanging lanterns and many other
uses. This lashing enables you to
make a tripod out of branches. Begin
the lash with a timber hitch, make
six to eight turns around all three
spars and finish up with two
binding turns between each spar.
Secure with a clove hitch on the
middle limb.

HOW TO MAKE A WHISTLE

THERE was once a time when every lad knew how to make his own whistle and the countryside echoed to the sound of their shrill blasts. A whistle is great for signalling, imitating birds and playing a merry tune, so get busy – it's time to rediscover the lost art of whistle-making!

YOU WILL NEED

- 10–15 cm (4–6 in) piece of willow or maple wood
- Sharp knife

1. Spring or early summer is the ideal time to find your piece of wood, as the rising sap will aid construction. Look for a branch of willow or maple tree that is straight and knot-free. The stick should be 10–15 cm (4–6 in) long and a little thicker than your thumb, but no more than about 2 cm (¾ in) in diameter.

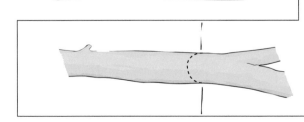

2. Cut the mouthpiece at an angle, leaving a small part of the end blunt so it isn't sharp in your mouth. Now cut a small notch through the bark about 2.5 cm (1 in) below the mouthpiece, until you slightly mark the wood itself. Cut the part of the notch closest to the mouthpiece by pressing straight down with your knife blade. Then cut the lower side of the notch with your knife at an angle towards the mouthpiece. Finally, score and remove a ring of bark about halfway down the stick.

3. Now you need to free the bark from the stick without damaging either. Give a sharp tap on the bark with the handle of your knife, but not so hard as to crack the bark, then gently tap all along the stick. When you're ready, firmly grip the stick with both hands and let one hand turn the bark, gently twisting it off in one piece. If the bark doesn't move, try tapping the stick again.

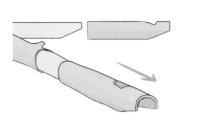

4. Find the mark on the stick where you cut out the notch in the bark and cut a deep notch into the wood. The deeper your notch, the lower the note your whistle will play, but don't make it too deep to begin with. Then remove a small sliver of wood between the deep notch and the mouthpiece.

5. Now dip your whistle into some water (or give it a good lick!) and slide the bark back on. Line up your bark exactly using the notch as your guide. Try blowing through the mouthpiece – you should hear a shrill note. If not, remove the bark again and experiment: extend the notch, make it deeper or cut a little more off the strip between the notch and the end. Now slip the bark back on and see if the result is any better.

WET YOUR WHISTLE

Your whistle will stop working if you allow it to dry out, so keep it outside or wrap it in a damp cloth. If you find it is dry, you can restore it to its original condition by soaking it in water.

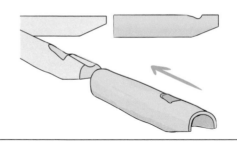

COLLECTING AND PURIFYING WATER

WHEN it comes to survival, water is the first and last truly essential requirement. Any adventurer should ensure they carry as much water with them as they can, but could you survive if you were stranded or lost?

COLLECTING WATER FROM PLANTS

No matter where you are, there is water around, even if it's just in the air. The secret is knowing how to tap into it. For example, in an emergency, plants can provide an excellent source of drinkable water.

To extract the moisture, find a plant with plenty of green foliage, but make sure it is alive, isn't poisonous and hasn't been sprayed with pesticide. Wrap a plastic bag or piece of plastic around the leaves and tie it tight. Arrange the plastic bag so that part of it is lower than the seal, either at the end of a branch for a tree, or in dips in the ground for a plant, and wait for four to five hours. Depending on the type of tree or plant and the prevailing conditions, you should be able to collect about a cupful of water in the bag.

BUILDING A SOLAR STILL

A solar still is simple to build and can provide around 1 l (2 pt) of water a day. The still collects water vapour on the underside of a plastic sheet, which condenses and drips into a cup. The end result is water that is cleaner than the purest rainwater.

YOU WILL NEED

- Spade or other digging tool
- Cup
- Plastic sheet
- Rocks

1. Look for a dip or a depression where rainwater might collect and dig a pit about 1.5 m (5 ft) wide and 1 m (3 ft) deep. Make a small hole in the centre of the pit and place the cup in it.
2. Cover the pit with the plastic sheet and anchor the corners with rocks, making sure moisture cannot escape.

3. Weigh the sheet down with a small rock and push it down so the sheet slopes into the centre of the pit at an angle. The lowest point of the sheet should now be just above the cup.
4. After a few hours, the cup should have collected enough water to drink. In especially dry conditions, placing vegetation inside the still can increase the amount of water collected.

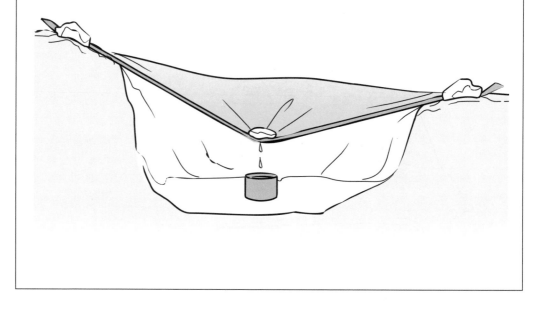

CAN YOU DRINK THE WATER?

Water is often freely available in the wild, but care should be taken to get it to a drinkable state. This will entail filtering and purifying.

To make a bottle filter: cut the bottom off a plastic bottle. Cut a clean sock in half and stuff one half as far down the neck of the bottle as you can. Add layers of sand and grass to a thickness of 2–3 cm (¾–1¼in) and then squeeze the second half of the sock into the bottle as the top layer. Pour your water through the filter until it is clear to the eye.

To make a tripod filter: build a tripod by lashing three sticks together, then fix two squares of clean cloth or handkerchiefs to it, one above the other. Put tiny pebbles in the top one. Place a saucepan below the bottom tier to collect the filtered water at the base.

Purifying water: filtering the water can remove detritus,

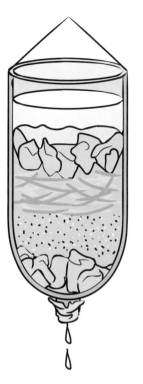

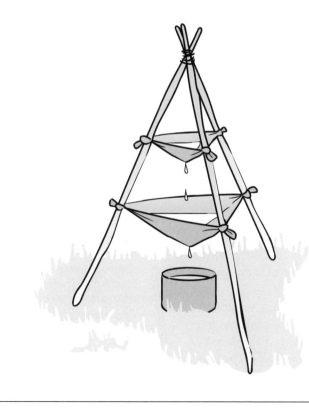

but it will not necessary make it drinkable. The simplest way of purifying water is simply to bring it to the boil. It doesn't need to boil for too long – five minutes or so should be enough to kill off any microbes or bacteria. The solar still also has the ability to purify tainted water as it condenses pure water from just about anything – even urine will produce clean, drinkable water.

MAKING A STRETCHER

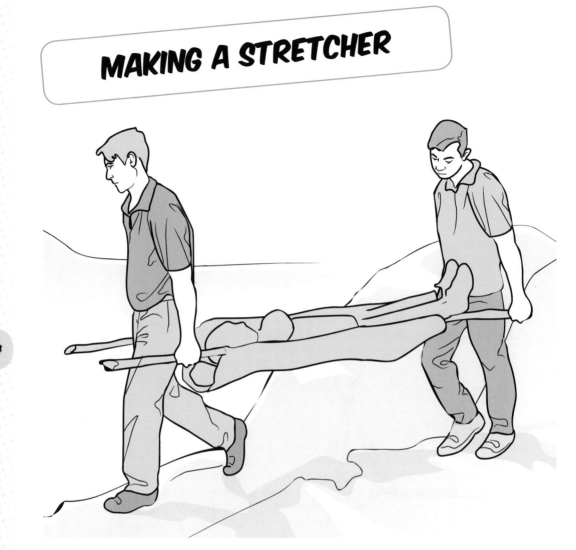

THE outdoor life can be thrilling and exciting, but there is a downside to that element of danger – injury. Any sensible adventurer is prepared for the eventuality of an accident and in an emergency will be able to fashion a makeshift stretcher.

Caution: improvised stretchers will not give sufficient support in cases where the casualty is suffering from fractures or extensive wounds to the body. They should be used only when the person is able to withstand bending, bumping or twisting without serious consequences.

YOU WILL NEED

- 2 wooden poles, about 2.5 m (8 ft) long and 5–10 cm (2–4 in) thick
- Large blanket or tarpaulin

THE BLANKET STRETCHER

Ensure the stretcher is carried by two people strong enough to bear the load and keep the injured person's bodyweight in the centre of the blanket.

1. Position the two poles in the centre of the blanket about 50 cm (20 in) apart.
2. Fold the left side over.
3. Fold the right side on top.

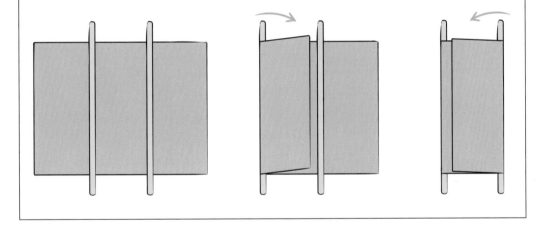

THE SHIRT STRETCHER

If you don't have a blanket to hand, try threading two shirts or two pairs of trousers on to your poles.

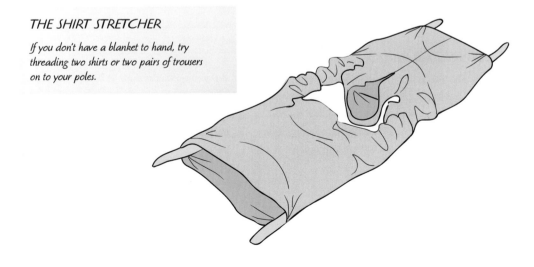

THE ROPE STRETCHER

It is also possible to use a rope to transport an injured person. You will need at least four people to take the weight and it will not be a comfortable journey for the casualty, so try cushioning the stretcher with strategically placed jumpers and shirts.

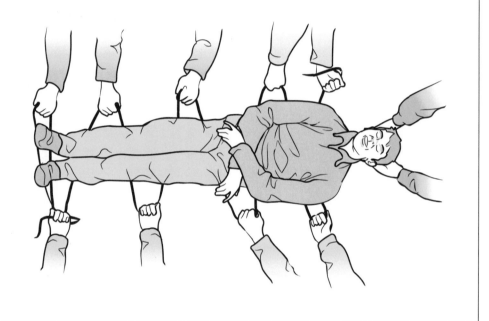

MOVING AN INJURED PERSON

- If the injury involves his or her neck or back, do not move the injured person, but fetch professional medical emergency services.
- If the person has to be dragged to safety, slide a coat or blanket under them and pull it gently lengthways.

- If the injured person must be lifted, use a board, table top or other firm surface to keep the injured person's body as level as possible. Support each part of the person's body, especially the head, as you lift.

HOW TO MAKE A CATAPULT

THE slingshot is a primitive weapon, but one that remains as simple and effective today as it's always been. Easy to make and use, it can be a lethal hunting weapon in a survival situation, but it's also great fun to shoot at targets when at camp. However, remember it can be extremely dangerous, so never aim it in the direction of people, animals or property.

YOU WILL NEED

- Y-shaped branch
- Knife
- 1 or 2 long, thick rubber bands or other stretchy, strong material
- Small piece of leather or cloth
- Small rubber bands

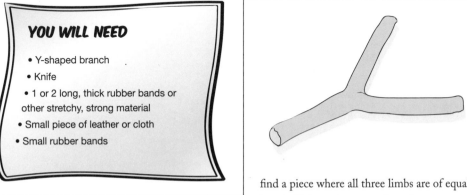

1. Find a sturdy, healthy Y-shaped branch about 15–25 cm (6–10 in) long, with a consistent thickness of around 3–4 cm (1¼–1½ in). Try to find a piece where all three limbs are of equal length. Trim and cut your branch to remove any knots and bumps and then peel and scrape away all the bark. Leave it to dry in a cool, dry place or in the sun.

2. Cut a long, thick rubber band in half or cut open two bands, to make two strips. Each strip should be around 15–20 cm (6–8 in) long.

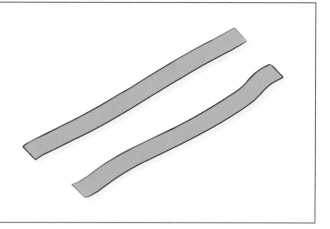

3. Take the leather or cloth which is going to form your 'pocket'. Cut a rectangular piece about 8 x 10 cm (3 x 4 in) and make a slit about 1 cm ($^1/_3$ in) in from each of the shorter edges, big enough for the rubber band to fit comfortably through.

4. Pass one end of a rubber band through the hole and fold it back to make a small loop around the edge of the pocket. Use a small rubber band to lash the strip closed. Do the same on the other side and make sure the bands on both sides are of equal length.

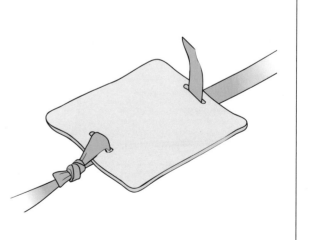

5. Now use more small rubber bands to secure the other ends of the long rubber bands to the catapult. Secure one of the long rubber bands to the back of one branch of the 'Y' and secure the other long rubber band to the back of the other branch. Make sure the bands are of equal length by pulling on the middle of the leather rectangle and seeing if it pulls more towards one side.

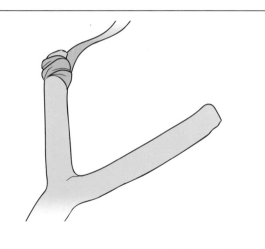

Your catapult is now complete. Break in the firing assembly by flexing the rubber strips to loosen them up. Then load a small berry or stone into the pocket – make sure no one is in the firing line – take aim and fire at your target. Enjoy your shooting!

MAKE A BOW AND ARROW

THINK you could have survived alongside Robin Hood and his Merry Men in Sherwood Forest? Not unless you were an expert archer, you couldn't. Being an expert, of course, meant being able to make your own bow and arrows, so here's how to do it – you'll be hitting a target at twenty paces in no time. I say target because what you are about to make can be a very dangerous weapon and should only ever be pointed at or used against a target – a bank of soft earth or sand if you want your arrows to survive. If, on the other hand, you find yourself in a desperate situation out in the wild, your bow and arrow is perfectly capable of helping you to bag a rabbit or other small animal – that is, once you've mastered the art of using it properly!

Now you are ready for target practice. You might want to wear a glove on your bow-hand to protect you from the string because it can really sting if it catches your wrist.

YOU WILL NEED

To make your bow and arrow you will need:

- Wooden staff about 1.5m (5ft) long and at least as thick as your thumb. Try to find or cut a straight length with few or no knots or offshoots. Yew is the traditional bow-making wood, but you can also use oak, elm, birch or just about any other strong, healthy wood
- As many straight, thin, 75cm (2 ft 6 in) lengths of wood as you would like for arrows
- Feathers (you can find them or maybe ask your local butcher) or some thin plastic card to use as flights
- Flint, bone, plastic or a tin can for the arrowhead
- Cord or twine
- Cotton thread
- Sharp knife
- Sharp scissors or tin snips

1. To make your bow bend and spring back so it can launch your arrows, you must first chamfer the ends. Mark the staff a third of the distance from each end, effectively dividing it into three sections. The end sections now need to be shaved along what will be the inside edge of the bow, tapering away towards the tip where they should end up about half the thickness of the middle section. Part of this chamfering may already have been achieved for you by the way the plant has grown.

2. Cut a thin groove in the unchamfered outside edge of the bow. The groove needs to be about 5cm (2 in) from the end. This is where you will tie your bow string.

3. Tie the cord or twine you are using as a bowstring to one end and bend the bow into a shallow arc (remember that it will have to bend a bit further when firing an arrow). Pull the bowstring tight and mark the length you need.

4. Tie a loop in the unfastened end of the bow. You should bend the bow and slip this loop over the end into its notch only when you intend to use the bow. Keeping it permanently strung will soon make your bow lose its springiness.

5. The front end of your arrow needs to be heavier than the back to stop the arrow cartwheeling through the air, so balance the arrow shaft on your finger like a see-saw to see which end is heavier – no naturally-grown stick is going to be uniform.

6. Carefully cut a slit in the lighter end and slip a feather in so that half the feather sticks out each side of the shaft. Bind some cotton thread around the shaft in front of and behind the feather to clamp the split closed and hold the feather in place. Instead of feathers, you can use a piece of thin plastic cut into a delta shape.

7. Cut a slit in the other end of the shaft to accept your arrowhead. You can make the arrowhead by pounding a piece of flint (take great care as flint shatters into razor-sharp shards), cutting a piece of triangular tin from your can, carving a piece of bone, or simply charring the end of the shaft in a fire to make it hard and then sharpening it.

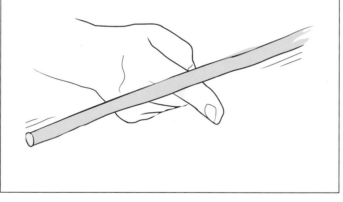

TRACKING

FOLLOWING the tracks of an animal is an intricate art that can take years to perfect. However, with a little practice you can determine which animals are in the vicinity and, if your tracking skills are good enough, they may even lead you straight to the animal itself.

The best kinds of terrain to find animal tracks are areas covered with wet sand, soft mud or new snow – on a beach, along riverbanks, in forests and woodland or near streams and lakes. The diagrams on these pages will help you identify which animal has left the tracks, but there are some general rules of thumb that can help you.

WHICH DIRECTION?

A creature's claw marks will point in the direction in which they were heading. If there are no claws, you will need to look for pushed back mud, dirt or snow, or bent grass, broken twigs and displaced pebbles.

IS IT CLOSE?

Tracks dry very quickly, especially in the sun, so try to judge their freshness. Also, animal droppings dry from the outside in, so the more moist the dropping, the nearer the animal.

TOES

- Four toes on each of the front and hind feet indicate the dog, cat or rabbit family.
- Small triangular marks in front of the paw print are claw marks. However, note that the cat family retract their claws when they run.
- Five toes each on the front and back feet point to the racoon and weasel family, which includes badgers, beavers, porcupines, otters, mink and bears.
- Four toes on the front foot and five on the rear means it's a rodent, usually mice, chipmunks, rats or squirrels.
- Two-toe tracks usually belong to a deer or elk.

Badger

YOU WILL NEED

- Strip of cardboard
- Plaster of Paris

COLLECTING TRACKS

1. Find a clear track and brush away any small stones, twigs and excess dirt.

2. Turn a cardboard strip into a collar by notching the ends together. Place the collar around the track and press it into the earth lightly. Mix up some plaster of Paris and pour it over the track until it is at least 2 cm (¾ in) thick.

3. Leave the plaster to harden for 10–15 minutes. Remove it and brush off the dirt. On the back of the cast, write the date and the place where you found the track.

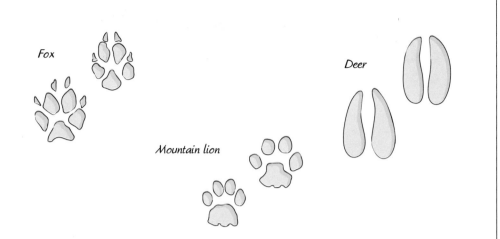

TRACK PATTERNS

Diagonal walkers: cats, dogs and hoofed animals lift their front and hind feet on opposite sides of the body at the same time, alternating sides as they go. This movement leaves a staggered set of tracks.

Gallopers: rabbits and squirrels bring their hind feet down in front and to the side of the front paws, which creates an easily recognized U-shaped track pattern. If the front feet hit a diagonal it is probably a rabbit, but if the front feet hit side by side it is a tree-dweller such as a squirrel.

Pacers: racoons, bears, beavers, porcupines, badgers and skunks usually move both feet on one side of the body at the same time in a shuffling or lumbering fashion.

Wolf

Bear

Wild boar

SECRET SIGNS AND MESSAGES

T HE ability to communicate through signs to others in the field – pals, team-mates, members of your party or strangers whom you can help on their way – is invaluable. It is, of course, possible to invent a series of signs among yourselves, which is useful if your movements need to be clandestine. But often you will have no opportunity to discuss such matters and will have to rely on your understanding of a common language, one that has been developed over hundreds of years.

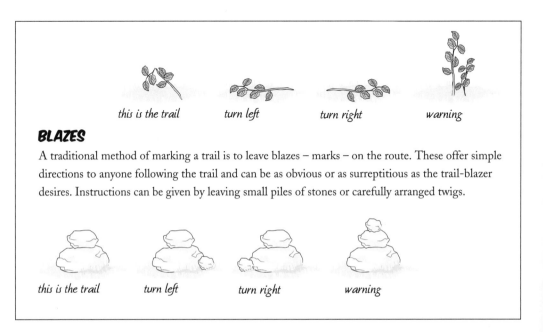

this is the trail   *turn left*   *turn right*   *warning*

BLAZES

A traditional method of marking a trail is to leave blazes – marks – on the route. These offer simple directions to anyone following the trail and can be as obvious or as surreptitious as the trail-blazer desires. Instructions can be given by leaving small piles of stones or carefully arranged twigs.

this is the trail   *turn left*   *turn right*   *warning*

THREE SIGNALS MEANS HELP!'

The universal sign for danger or help, recognized by most rovers and rangers, is three signals delivered consecutively. A chap in trouble and requiring assistance should issue three shouts, three whistles, three shots from a gun or – at night – three flashes of a torch. Anyone seeing such signals should try to ascertain the position of the person needing assistance and seek help immediately.

SMOKE SIGNALS

Smoke signals are associated with Native North Americans, but they have been used around the world for centuries. Their great advantage is that if the sending fire is built on a high place, they can be seen over great distances. Smoke signals are sent by holding a cover, such as a blanket, a few feet above a smouldering fire. Grass and branches are added to the fire to create a great deal of smoke and puffs of smoke are issued by moving the blanket to one side for a short time and then replacing it. Smoke signals are an ideal medium for secret messages, but there are some universal signals:

• One puff – attention
• Two puffs – all's well
• Three puffs – danger or trouble

TRAMPS' SIGNS

Over many years, tramps and those who live on the open road have developed their own markings to help out fellow itinerants. These signs often relate to the friendliness or otherwise of the landowner, or whether it is fertile begging territory. However, many of their signs can be utilized by today's outdoorsmen. Here are a few that you might come across or that you might like to adopt.

Safe camp

Sleep in barn

Here is the place

Help if sick

Man with a gun

Camp here

Turn right here

Turn left here

Danger

TRAPS AND SNARES

FINDING food in an extreme survival situation is one of the toughest challenges an adventurer can face. As it is unlikely you will gather sufficient nuts and berries for your survival, it could be imperative that you know how to trap animals for food.

Caution: the trapping techniques described here are strictly for wilderness survival situations. Setting traps and snares is often illegal. Please be aware of any local hunting rules and trapping regulations.

YOU WILL NEED

- Wire
- Wire cutters or pliers
- A sharp knife for cutting branches, etc.

TRAPPING TIPS

- Increase your chances of a catch by setting as many traps and snares as you are able.
- Check your traps regularly to prevent both escape and undue suffering.
- Set traps on animal trails (see Tracking on page 113) or in gaps between rocks or in hedges.
- Hide your scent. Wear gloves when handling the trap, or hold the snaring material over smoke or under water for a couple of minutes.

MAKING TRAPS AND SNARES

The following traps can all be constructed with some wire and whatever materials you can find around. Select the trap with a mind as to what animals might be in the area and take great care not to snare yourself!

Deadfall: A deadfall is a baited trap which, when triggered, allows a weight to drop on the animal, hopefully killing it immediately or at least incapacitating it. The trigger is a figure 4 composed of three notched sticks. The two forming the cross – when used for rabbit-sized animals – will each be about 15 cm (6 in) long, and the prop stick about 20 cm (8 in) (the sizes will vary according to the type of animal to be trapped). The weight is usually a large, flattish rock or a log.

The trap requires care and patience to assemble as the notches hold the sticks together in a figure 4 pattern under delicate tension. When assembling it, ensure the vertical stake is not positioned beneath the rock or log, and the bait on the crosspiece is as far under the weight as is practical. The trap should also be placed on hard ground or a rock so the deadfall doesn't just press the animal into soft ground.

Tripwire deadfall: This version of the Deadfall provides a tripwire that can be drawn across a well-used animal trail or run. First, secure two short pegs into a tree trunk and find a stick to use as a bar between them. Keep the pegs as short as possible so that the bar will disengage easily.

Wrap the wire around the log or rock to be used as the deadfall, then pass it under the bar and peg it out across the trail. The prey will disturb the wire, dislodge the bar and the deadfall will come crashing down.

Spring snare: The trigger for the spring snare is made with two notched sticks. The longer stick is pushed into the ground and the shorter one is held against it by the upward pull of a bent sapling or branch. The noose is tied to the small stick and suspended over the run at head height so that when the animal comes by, it pushes its head through the noose and dislodges the trigger stick.

The upward pressure of the tree will tighten the noose and pull the animal suddenly up into the air when released. Remember though, some trees and branches, if left bent over for too long, will lose some of their spring and become much less effective.

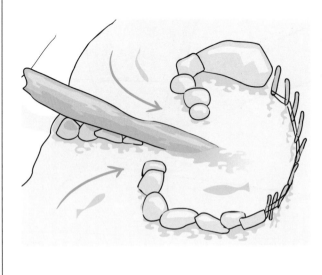

Fish funnel trap: Fish swim next to banks at night or move from deep holes into shallow water to feed. They can often be directed into traps from which they are unlikely to escape by placing an obstruction across the water. The walls of the trap are made with piled-up stones or tightly-spaced sticks driven solidly into the river or lakebed.

When you have enough fish in the enclosure, close the entrances to the trap.

HOW TO CATCH A RABBIT IN A HOLE

A FIELDSMAN in need of a square meal should look no further than the humble bunny. Rabbits aren't too hard to catch, are easy to skin and can be delicious cooked over the campfire.

This technique relies on a rabbit's tendency not to retreat too far down a hole and its defence mechanism of freezing when threatened. Sometimes you can see a rabbit with a torch or a mirror and almost reach in and grab it, but unfortunately they usually lurk just beyond your reach – which is when you'll need your rabbit stick.

1. Find a long, flexible branch, as straight as possible and around 1 m (3 ft) or so in length.

2. Jab one end against hard ground or a tree trunk until it splits into sharp ends.

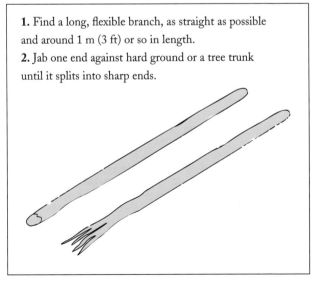

RABBIT STARVATION

Although rabbits are relatively easy to catch, and as tasty as they are, a chap cannot survive on rabbit alone. Rabbit starvation occurs because the meat is so lean that you can eat as much as you like, but still die of malnutrition. So somehow you need to make sure that your survival diet includes at least some fat and, ideally, carbohydrate.

3. Stand still and look around until you spot a rabbit disappearing down a hole.

4. Carefully push your rabbit stick down the hole until you feel it gently strike the rabbit. Slowly, try to slide the stick under it.

5. Gently twist the stick so that it catches on the rabbit's fur. Then continue twisting until you feel your stick has got a good grip on it

6. Slowly pull the rabbit out and grab it by the ears with your other hand.

THE OJIBWA BIRD POLE

FOR the hungry wilderness survivor, a bird can make a good meal. All species of birds are edible, although the flavour does vary. However, trying to catch such elusive creatures can prove frustrating. This bird pole snare is named after the Native North American tribe who used it for centuries.

Caution: the unnecessary hunting of birds is cruel and is illegal in many countries of the world. Certain species of birds are also protected by law in some countries.

WHERE TO SET THE SNARE

Knowing where birds nest and when they fly will help you position your snare. Birds tend to have regular flyways going from the roost to a feeding area or to water. Find a relatively open area away from tall trees along this route and set the snare. Birds should naturally seek out the perch, but you can adjust the sensitivity of the 'trigger' to avoid catching birds that are too small.

YOU WILL NEED

- 2 m (6 ft 6 in) long pole
- Sharp knife
- Drill
- 15 cm (6 in) stick
- Short length of cord
- Small rock

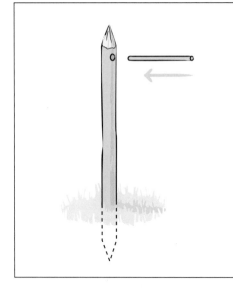

1. Sharpen both ends of the pole and drill a small hole through one end. Drive the other end into the ground until it is secure. Fit the stick loosely into the hole.

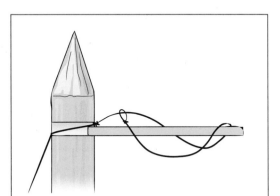

2. Pass a cord through the hole in the pole, then make a slip noose that drapes over the perch. If the noose is blown off by the wind use a little spittle to fasten it down.

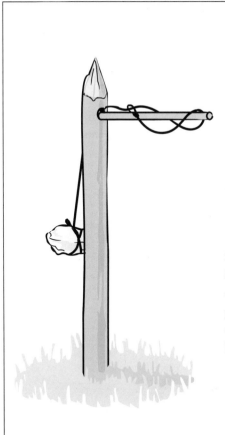

3. Tie a rock to the other end of the cord. Tie a knot in the cord at the back of the noose and place the stick against the hole, letting the tension hold it in place. When a bird flies down and perches, it will displace the stick, the rock will fall and its feet will be caught as the loop quickly slides through the hole.

HOW TO FISH

T HE art of fishing has everything the outdoor chap could wish for: a relaxing fresh-air pastime in idyllic settings; a skill that can always be practised and perfected; moments of action and excitement; and, of course, something delicious to cook on the campfire at the end of the day.

YOU WILL NEED

- Fishing rod with a reel
- Line and hooks
- Weights
- Bait
- Floats

1. The cinch knot is utilized by anglers across the world to attach their line to a hook. It's easy to tie and can be used even if you just have a stick and a bent safety pin to fish with. Pass the line through the eye of the hook. Double back and make five turns around the standing line.

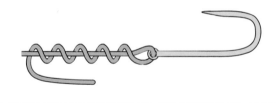

2. Holding the turns in place, thread the tag end of the first loop above the eye and then through the big loop.

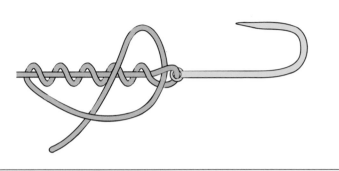

3. Hold the tag end and standing line while pulling up the loops. Make sure the loops are in a spiral, not overlapping each other. Slide against the eye and clip the tag end.

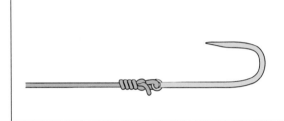

4. Clip one or two weights to the line about 25 cm (10 in) above the hook. This weight will keep your bait in the water and will help swing it away from shore.

5. The simplest bait is a worm. Wind it around the hook and push the hook through the worm, until the hook is mostly covered. If your worm is still alive and wriggling then all the better.

6. The novice fisherman will seldom feel when a fish is nibbling at his bait, so place your float about 50 cm (20 in) from the hook and remember to keep watching – if you see it bobbing you might well have a bite.

7. Casting is the art of placing your line in the water. Stand with your feet and shoulders facing the water. Point the rod at right angles to the body aiming at an object on the horizon. Reel in the line so the hook hangs a few centimetres (an inch or so) from the tip of the rod and hold the rod at the handle with one hand or two, thumb on the reel.

8. Check the immediate area around and above to ensure you have space to cast. Move the rod to point it slightly behind the shoulder of the casting arm, at 11 o'clock. Your elbows should be at 90 degrees and your hands slightly above and in front of the shoulder. With the thumb of your casting arm, push and hold the button on the reel.

9. Rotate the wrist, extend the arm forward and snap the rod back to the 3 o'clock position. When your arm reaches the 'half past one' position, release your thumb from the reel button.

If the line went too high and fell short you released the button too soon. If the line went too low and fell short you released the button too late.

When you have cast, give the reel a turn and take up the slack. The waiting game has begun…

10. When your float goes completely under water, lower the rod tip, wind up any slack line and sharply jerk the rod upwards. Keep the line tight so the fish can't shake the hook loose. It's possible to land many small fish just by reeling them in, but some put up more of a fight. Keeping the line taut at all times, pull the rod up to the 11 o'clock position, then reel in the line quickly as you lower the rod until it is horizontal and pointed at the fish. Repeat the process until the fish is near and ready to be landed.

HOW TO CATCH CRABS BY HANDLINE

WITH just some bait and a length of string, a chap can have himself an exhilarating time. Catching crabs with a handline is strictly a recreational activity, but it's simple, inexpensive and provides all-day fun.

YOU WILL NEED

- 2 m (6ft 6 in) length of string
- 25–30 cm (9–12 in) long stick
- A weight – a small stone or heavy nut and bolt
- Bait – raw chicken necks or fish heads are the most effective
- Pole fishing net
- Bucket for your catch
- Gloves for handling the crabs

WHERE TO CATCH CRABS

Find a bridge, pier or dock when the tide is rising. You'll need at least 2 m (6 ft 6 in) of water; basically, the deeper the water the better.

1. Tie a stick on to one end of your length of string and attach a weight and a piece of your bait securely to the other end.

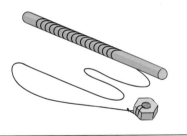

2. Drop your bait into the water, holding your stick tightly. Check the line carefully by pulling it up with your thumb and forefinger – this will help you feel any movement. Wait for the tug of the crab eating your bait.

3. If you feel a nibble, slowly raise the line to the surface. Trying not to scare the crab, gently reel in your line, wrapping it around your stick until the crab hangs in the air. Although the crab is usually so busy eating that it is unaware it is being pulled from the bottom, avoid sharp movements and be patient.

4. Keep the line tight and pull the string up slowly and steadily. When you can see the crab near the surface of the water, get your net ready and as soon as you can, scoop it up.

133

HOW TO HANDLE A LIVE CRAB

Wear gloves! Keep the crab still by pressing lightly on its top shell with a stick. Place a thumb on top of the claw where it meets the shell and a forefinger underneath where it meets the underbody. All your other fingers should be closed into the palm of your hand to keep them out of the way of nipping claws.

HOW TO TICKLE A TROUT

IS it possible to catch a trout by tickling it? Many swear it is and claim to have done it, but many others have tried and just ended up with a cold, wet hand. So, if you're the kind of fellow who appreciates a challenge, step to it.

YOU WILL NEED

- Steady hand
- Great deal of patience
- Lots of luck

1. Pick a stream that you know contains trout and find a secure, overhanging rock. Lie down on it and slowly ease your hand into the water from the downstream side.

2. Once you have a target in sight and moving as slowly as you can, bring your hand forward until you are touching the trout's tail. Grit your teeth and pray that it won't dart away.

3. Put your thumb and forefinger on either side of the trout's tail and gently caress the trout on both sides.

4. Slowly work your way along the trout's body, tickling gently with both digits.

5. When your hand is just behind the gills, squeeze the fish, pull it forwards and throw it on to the shore.

HOW TO GUT AND CLEAN A FISH

A FISH is one of nature's great convenience foods – the hardest part is catching the flighty fellow. However, once it's on the fire, you'll soon have a delicious meal, but first you'll have to deal with the messy stuff…. You'll need plenty of water, so why not stay by the river and do it there and then?

YOU WILL NEED

- A fish
- Water
- Sharp knife
- Board
- Rubbish bag
- Spoon

1. To kill the fish, either hit it just behind the head with a blunt, solid object, or grab it firmly by the tail and swing it against something hard. Now wash the fish thoroughly with running or under water.

FISH-GUTTING TIPS

- *Gut any fish longer than 10 cm (4 in).*
- *Gut fish as soon as possible after you catch them.*
- *If you can bear it, bleed the fish while it is still alive by slicing through the tail until the knife touches bone and letting the blood flow out.*
- *Avoid soaking cleaned fish fillets in water for too long as this could adversely affect the texture and flavour of the meat.*

2. Take a sharp knife and remove the little fins on either side of the body. Now lay the fish flat on its side and to see if it needs scaling, run the back of a knife at nearly a 90° angle all along the body. If the knife passes smoothly over the scales, move to the next step. If the scales pop up and are quite thick then, using short strokes, scrape from the tail to the head until the fish is smooth. Now wash off any clinging scales.

3. Lie the fish on the board with the tail furthest away from you. Holding the tail, insert your knife into the small opening by the underside of the tail fin and cut away a thin strip (0.5 cm/¼ in) of skin all the way along the belly up to the gills. Discard this.

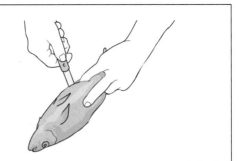

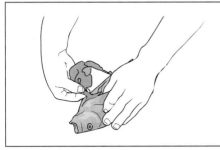

4. Using your fingers, dig around a bit and remove the guts from the cavity. Now using a spoon or the tip of your knife, scoop out the red kidney line along the fish's spine. Give the fish a thorough rinse.

5. Cut lightly into the skin either side of the dorsal fin on top of the fish and give it a swift tug, from the tail end outwards. It should bring most of the bones with it. Now remove the head just below the gills, and the tail where it joins the body. Your fish should now be ready to cook.

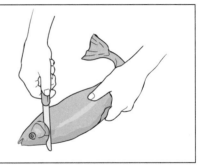

CUNNING INVENTIONS

MAKE A TIN CAN TELEPHONE

AN improvised telephone set made out of tin cans – are you sure? Would you believe you can chat to your chums down a line made of string? Have a go at this fun activity and you'll find you have to believe your own ears!

YOU WILL NEED

- Hammer and a thick nail
- 2 empty clean, dry metal cans with the lids removed (take care not to leave any sharp edges)
- 3–4 m (10–13 ft) thin cotton string

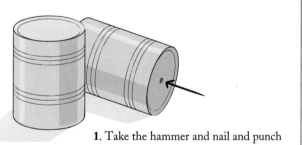

1. Take the hammer and nail and punch a small hole in the bottom of each can. Each hole should be just large enough so that the string will go through.

2. From the outside, insert one end of the string into the hole in one can. Tie a couple of knots in the end of the string so that it won't slip back through when pulled tight. Do the same with the other end of the string and the other can.

3. With one person holding each can, stretch the string so that it is taut. You'll find that if you talk into a can, the other fellow, by putting his ear to the other can, will be able to hear what you're saying.

Don't try listening around corners, though. If your string comes into contact with a brick wall or a door, the sound will be lost and never reach the other can.

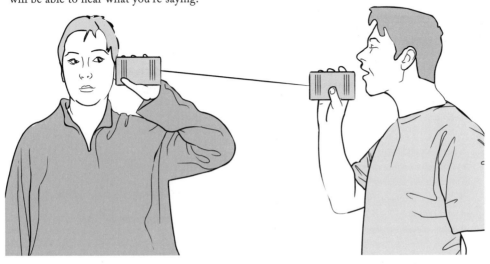

MAKE A WATER-POWERED ROCKET

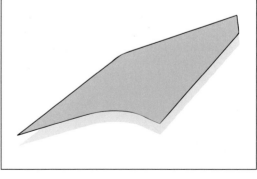

SEND a rocket into space and get your chums wet at the same time – what could be more fun? This rocket works on the same principle as real rockets – Newton's Third Law of Motion, which states that for every action there is an equal and opposite reaction. So what are you waiting for? Rocket science has never been so not rocket science!

YOU WILL NEED

- Sheet of polystyrene
- Scissors or a sharp hobby knife
- Adhesive tape
- Empty 2 l (4 pt) plastic bottle
- Cork
- Hammer and large nail
- Inflating valve (the needle type used to inflate basketballs or footballs)
- Air pump (bicycle pump, foot pump or stand pump)
- Protective eye goggles

1. Trace out the shape of four identical fins on the polystyrene, using the base of the bottle as a guide for the curved edge. Cut them out with the knife or scissors.

2. Use the tape to attach the fins to the plastic bottle as shown.

3. Hammer the nail through the centre of the cork and then remove it. Push the inflating valve through the hole made by the nail. It should fit tightly.

4. Fill the bottle about a third full of water. Push the cork and valve into the bottle opening.

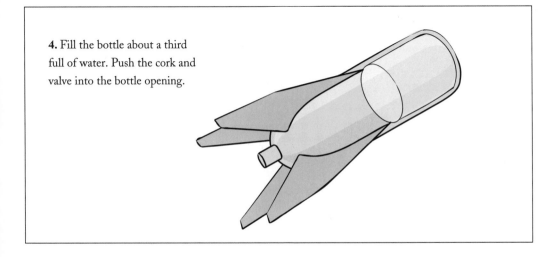

5. This next step is a two-person job. Find an open space, away from people, animals and buildings. One person holds the rocket and the other pumps. Attach the pump to the valve and turn the bottle so the fins are at the base. At this point both the person holding the rocket and the person pumping air into the bottle should put on some protective eye goggles. Start to operate the pump. The further the cork was pushed into the bottle, the longer you will have to pump, but it will be worth it. Unfortunately you won't be able to do a countdown, since there is no way of telling exactly when the rocket will launch.

6. The rocket will take off – spurting water from the bottom as the cork is expelled.

TIP

To make your rocket fly straighter, try taping two or three coins to the top of it.

BUILD A GLIDER

YOU WILL NEED

- 2 pieces of balsa wood: piece A 30 x 1 x 0.6 cm (12 x ⅓ x ¼ in); piece B 60 x 3.5 x 0.3 cm (24 x 1¼ x ⅛ in)
- Ruler
- Craft knife
- Sandpaper
- Wood glue
- Rubber bands
- Small piece of Plasticine (modelling clay)

MOST chaps have dreamed (usually in the middle of a lesson or a meeting!) of launching the perfect model aeroplane, one that glides away on the thermals and gracefully descends to earth. This plane won't do that. Not immediately. But sort out your aerodynamics and adjust the launch angle, wing position and nose weight – and you might just achieve that perfect flight.

1. Piece A will form the fuselage. Mark and cut out all the other required elements from piece B:

One wing – 27 x 3.5 cm
(10¾ x 1¼ in)

One horizontal stabilizer –
8 x 2.5 cm (3 x 1 in)

One vertical stabilizer –
3.5 x 2.5 cm (1¼ x 1 in)

Three wing mounting pieces –
6 x 0.3 cm (2¼ x ⅛ in)

2. Cut the wing down to the dimensions shown. Sand all of the pieces so they are smooth to the touch.

27 cm (10¾ in)

10.5 cm
(4¹/₁₀ in)

6 cm
(2²/₅ in)

10.5 cm
(4¹/₁₀ in)

2 cm (¾ in)

3. Using glue, assemble the wing mount in a 'U' shape as shown in the diagram.

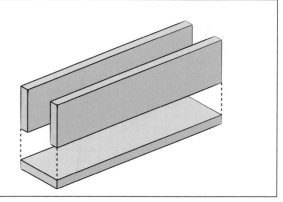

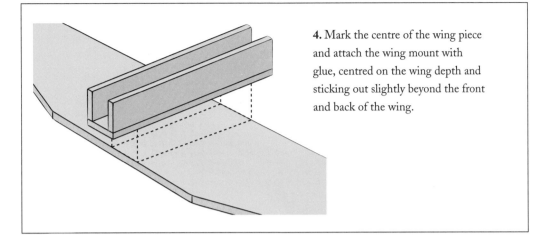

4. Mark the centre of the wing piece and attach the wing mount with glue, centred on the wing depth and sticking out slightly beyond the front and back of the wing.

5. Mount the horizontal stabilizer so it fits flush with the end of the fuselage. Then mount the vertical stabilizer so it forms a right angle to the horizontal piece.

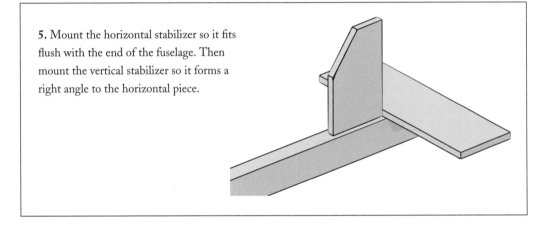

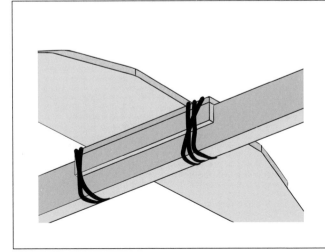

6. Secure the wing 12 cm (4¾ in) from the front of the fuselage by wrapping rubber bands around both sides of the wing mounting and the fuselage.

7. Add a small piece of Plasticine (modelling clay) to the front of the fuselage, to form the nose.

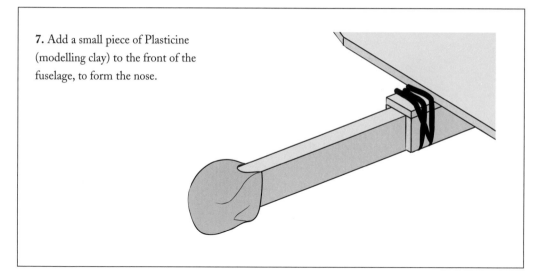

8. It's now time for a test flight. Find an open stretch of land, hold your hand under the fuselage and partially under the wing, and throw it straight ahead with a firm and smooth action. Adjust the nose weight (i.e. the amount of Plasticine) until the plane flies level. Similarly, if the plane pitches to the left or the right add a small piece of Plasticine to the opposite wing.

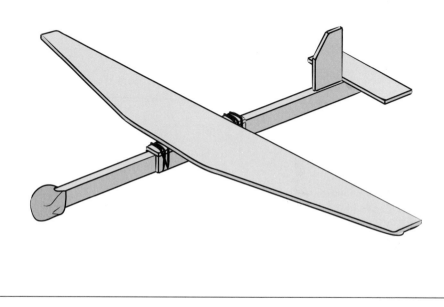

BUILD YOUR OWN GO-KART

IT may not look sleek or powerful, but when you've built this go-kart with your own fair hands you'll be as proud as punch. And when you're careering down the hill on it, not knowing whether to scream with fear or sheer exhilaration, there will be a part of your brain working on whether a small adjustment could make it go just that little bit faster…

Go-karts are traditionally made from scrap materials, so the design of yours will depend on what you can find, but this plan should give you enough first principles to build your own unique vehicle.

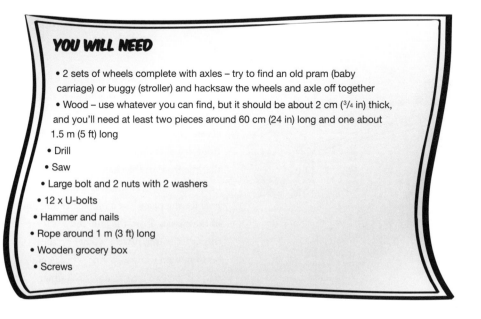

YOU WILL NEED

- 2 sets of wheels complete with axles – try to find an old pram (baby carriage) or buggy (stroller) and hacksaw the wheels and axle off together
- Wood – use whatever you can find, but it should be about 2 cm (³/₄ in) thick, and you'll need at least two pieces around 60 cm (24 in) long and one about 1.5 m (5 ft) long
- Drill
- Saw
- Large bolt and 2 nuts with 2 washers
- 12 x U-bolts
- Hammer and nails
- Rope around 1 m (3 ft) long
- Wooden grocery box
- Screws

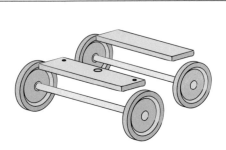

1. For the front wheels, cut a piece of wood to the same length as the axle. Cut a groove in which the axle can sit. This must be slightly forward of the centre of the wood as the pivot bolt needs to go through the middle. Drill a large hole for the pivot bolt to go through, and two smaller holes for the rope. Repeat the process for the back wheels, but this time the axle can be placed in the centre of the wood and you don't need the holes for the pivot bolt or rope.

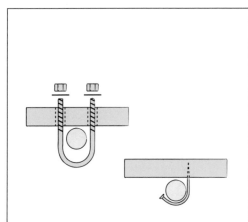

2. Now fix the axles to the wood. Use about a dozen bent-over nails to hold the axles to the wood. If you can get hold of some U-bolts these will do the same job much more securely.

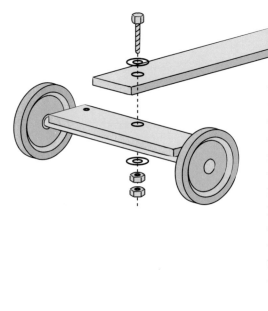

3. Now fit the chassis to the front wheel assembly. The chassis should be two-thirds of the length of your legs. Mark out the centre line of the board and position the front wheel assembly under the plank so that the front of the chassis extends a little beyond the wheels. Mark and then drill the hole for the pivot bolt along the centre line of the chassis. Push the bolt and a washer through the top, place a washer on the bottom, then using a spanner at each end, tighten the two nuts against each other.

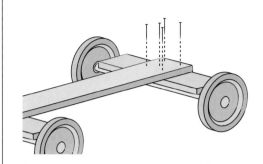

4. Mount the back wheel assembly by positioning it at the very back of the chassis. Make sure it is centred, then screw or nail from the top down to fix it securely in place.

5. Attach a steering rope through the holes in the near corners of the front wheel assembly. Tie large knots underneath to prevent the rope from pulling up through the holes.

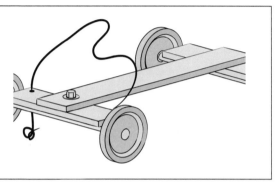

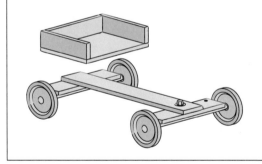

6. Sit on the kart with your feet on the front wheel assembly and mark where your seat should be. Nail down a grocery box with one side removed or build a small three-sided box (as pictured) for your seat.

Take your karting steadily at first, until you get used to the steering, but it won't be long before you're racing along in training for your first soapbox derby!

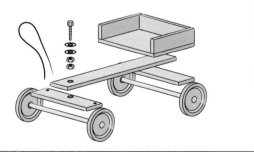

MAKE AN EXPLODING LOLLY STICK FRISBEE

THE chap who can fashion a pastime with whatever he finds to hand will never be at a loss. Memorize this piece of handicraft and, whatever company you find yourself in, not only will they think you an intrepid sort, but you'll keep them all well amused too.

YOU WILL NEED

• 5 lolly (popsicle) sticks

1. Take two of your lolly sticks, with the flat sides facing you, and make a V shape with them.

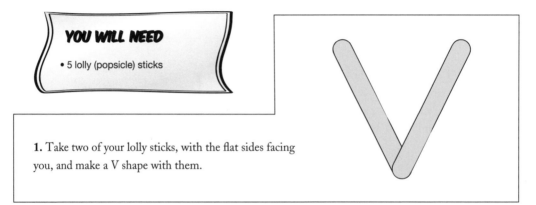

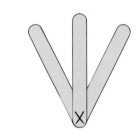

2. Hold the base of the V between your thumb and forefinger. With your other hand, take the third stick and wedge it into the middle of the V, on top of the other two, so your thumb and finger are now gripping all three.

3. With your other hand, take the fourth stick and weave it between the others. It should be above the middle stick and below the outer sticks. Push it about halfway down the V.

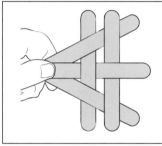

4. Take the last stick and weave it the opposite way to the previous one. The sticks will bend a little, but take care not to break them.

5. You should now be able to grasp the frisbee at one of the corners and it should hold together on its own. Push the top stick as close to the top edge of the device as you can without it flying off. This will aid the force of the explosion.

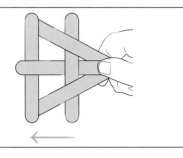

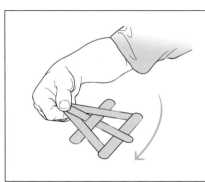

6. Now, hold the lolly stick frisbee at its base and throw it just as you would throw a real one. Either in flight or when it hits the ground, it will 'explode' with the sticks flying in all directions. Please have a care, though, and avoid throwing the frisbee at people, pets or property.

MAKE A WATER BOMB

ON a scorching hot day no one really minds some watery devilment and these little paper chappies are one of the easiest ways to get the fun going. You'll need to be a dab hand at the old paper-folding, but as soon as you get the gist of it, you'll be public enemy number one around camp!

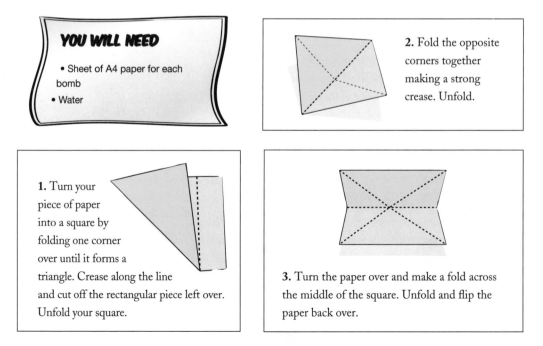

YOU WILL NEED

- Sheet of A4 paper for each bomb
- Water

2. Fold the opposite corners together making a strong crease. Unfold.

1. Turn your piece of paper into a square by folding one corner over until it forms a triangle. Crease along the line and cut off the rectangular piece left over. Unfold your square.

3. Turn the paper over and make a fold across the middle of the square. Unfold and flip the paper back over.

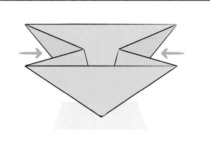

4. Push both sides inward and bring the bottom half up. You should be left with an upside-down triangle.

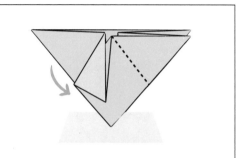

5. Hold the two front top corners and fold them down to the point at the bottom.

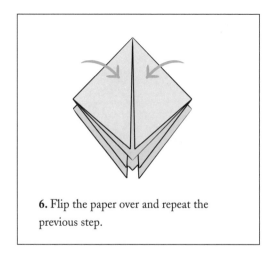

6. Flip the paper over and repeat the previous step.

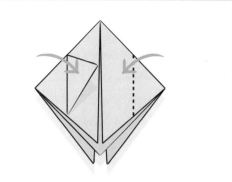

7. Fold the right and left corners so their points meet at the centre.

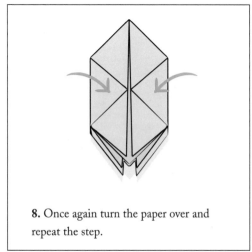

8. Once again turn the paper over and repeat the step.

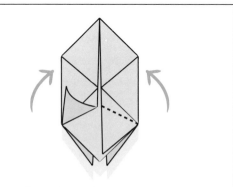

9. Bring the two bottom points up and make a firm fold where they meet the middle triangles.

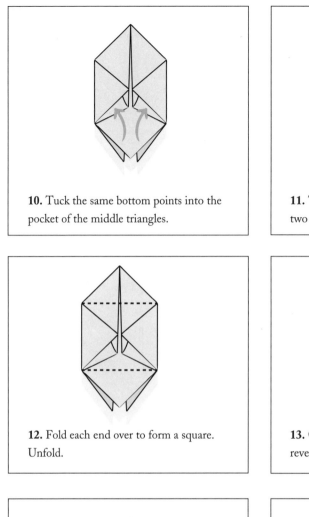

10. Tuck the same bottom points into the pocket of the middle triangles.

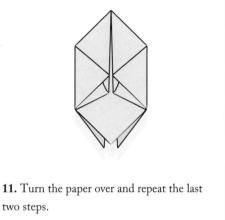

11. Turn the paper over and repeat the last two steps.

12. Fold each end over to form a square. Unfold.

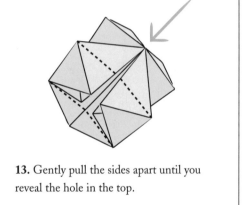

13. Gently pull the sides apart until you reveal the hole in the top.

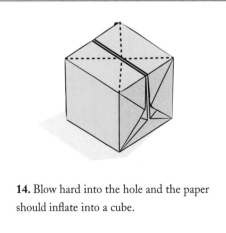

14. Blow hard into the hole and the paper should inflate into a cube.

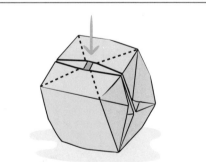

15. Pour some water through the hole in the top until the cube fills up. Look around for an unsuspecting victim (hoping they haven't read this book too)!

HOW TO MAKE A POPGUN

CALL it idle amusement or put it down to a love of japes and larks, but inside every lad there is an ability to wile away hours with a realistic popgun. This intriguing, simple-to-make 'weapon' not only gives a satisfying 'pop' but actually fires a real cork, too. Just get yourself a stetson and go get 'em cowboy!

YOU WILL NEED

- 30 cm (12 in) white PVC plastic pipe, 2 cm (³/₄ in) in diameter (available from hardware stores and plumbing suppliers)
- 40 cm (16 in) wooden dowel, 2 cm (³/₄ in) in diameter
- Hacksaw
- Scissors
- Polystyrene sheet or a supermarket vegetable packaging tray
- Adhesive tape
- Screwdriver and 2 cm (³/₄ in) long screw
- String
- Cork

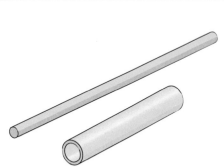

1. If the dowel and PVC pipe that you have bought or found are longer than required, use a hacksaw to cut them to the right length. Make the cuts as straight as possible.

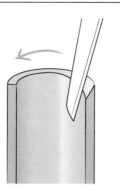

2. Push one blade of your scissors 1 cm (½ in) or so into the pipe and scrape around the inside. Small curled pieces of plastic should come away and you'll create a sharpened, bevelled end where the opening is wider than the inside of the tube.

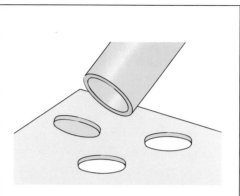

3. With the sharpened end of the pipe, push and twist out three seals from the polystyrene sheet.

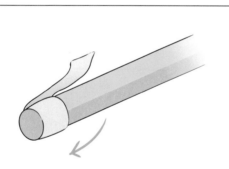

4. Wrap some adhesive tape around one end of the dowel, but make sure it will still fit through the pipe.

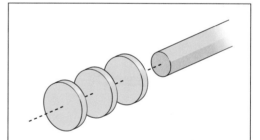

5. Screw through the centres of the three polystyrene seals into the centre of the other end of the dowel. Continue to turn the screw until its head makes a slight indent in the first seal.

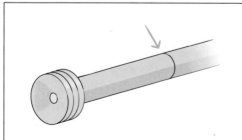

6. Make a mark on the dowel 7 cm (2¾ in) from the sealed end. Then slide the other end of the dowel into the bevelled end of the pipe. When the dowel emerges at the other end of the pipe, pull the seals just into the pipe, but no further.

7. Pull the dowel out until you get to the mark. Keeping the dowel in that position, tape one end of your string to the pipe and the other end of the string to the end of the dowel, making sure the string is tight so the dowel cannot come all the way out. Where the string is taped to the dowel, continue wrapping tape around there until the bulge is so big it doesn't fit into the pipe any more.

8. Now load your gun. Push a cork into the open end of the gun. You may need to twist it to get it in or you might have to bevel the cork as you did the pipe in step 2.

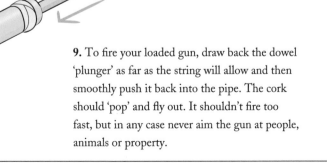

9. To fire your loaded gun, draw back the dowel 'plunger' as far as the string will allow and then smoothly push it back into the pipe. The cork should 'pop' and fly out. It shouldn't fire too fast, but in any case never aim the gun at people, animals or property.

MAKE A RUBBER BAND-POWERED BOAT

ANY small pond or big puddle seems to be crying out for a toy boat to venture across its treacherous waters and you seem just the man to provide one. This simple-to-make rubber band boat will put you in charge of your own vessel, but take it easy skipper and watch out for those lily pads!

YOU WILL NEED

- 25 x 12.5 cm (10 x 5 in) rectangle of polystyrene or wood, 2 cm (³⁄₄ in) thick
- 15 x 5 cm (6 x 2 in) rectangle of polystyrene or wood, 0.5 cm (¹⁄₄ in) thick
- Craft knife or small saw
- Glue
- Acrylic paints and brushes
- 2 small nails or drawing pins
- Small hammer
- Rubber bands

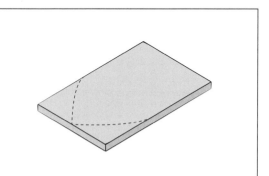

1. Using the 25 x 12.5 cm (10 x 5 in) rectangle of polystyrene or wood, shape one of the shorter ends so that it resembles the bow (front) of a boat.

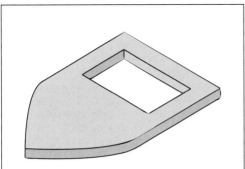

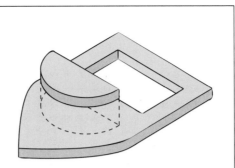

2. Starting 3.75 cm (1½ in) in from the opposite end, cut a 10 x 7.5 cm (4 x 3 in) opening for the paddle wheel.

3. From the piece you've just removed, cut a semicircle block (7.5 cm/3 in long at the flat end) to make a cabin. Glue this to the centre of the bow of the boat.

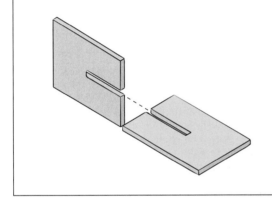

4. Cut the rectangle of thin polystyrene or wood in half to make two 7.5 x 5 cm (3 x 2 in) rectangles. Make a notch, 2.5 x 0.75 cm (1 x ⅓ in), in the centre of each of them. Fit the two pieces together to form a cross. This will be your paddle wheel.

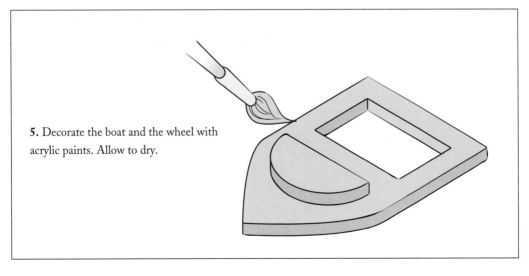

5. Decorate the boat and the wheel with acrylic paints. Allow to dry.

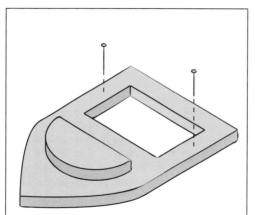

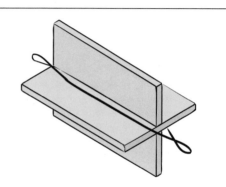

6. Tap a small drawing pin or nail partway into the boat on each side of the wheel opening.

7. Tie knots at each end of a rubber band to form two small loops, then place a loop around each nail and fit the middle of the band around the middle of the paddle wheel. Place the wheel in the opening and pass the loops over the pins.

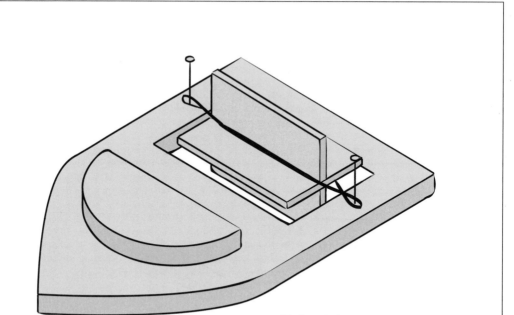

8. To launch the boat, turn the wheel until the rubber band is tightly twisted, place the boat in the water, release the wheel and watch the boat go. Happy boating!

MAKE A HOT-AIR BALLOON

THIS activity may take some time and is a little fiddly in places, but it will all seem worthwhile when you watch your balloon float up, up and away into the sky. Have your running shoes on though, because the balloon will go wherever the wind takes it and you could find yourself chasing it for a couple of miles.

YOU WILL NEED

- 8 sheets of tissue paper, 120 x 30 cm (47 x 12 in) (glue smaller sheets together if necessary)
- Scissors
- Stiff card
- Paper glue
- 45 cm (18 in) flexible wire (an old wire coat-hanger will do)
- 3 empty tin cans (all the same size)
- Tin opener
- Adhesive tape
- Campfire
- 20 cm (8 in) string
- Stick or broom handle at least 30 cm (12 in) long

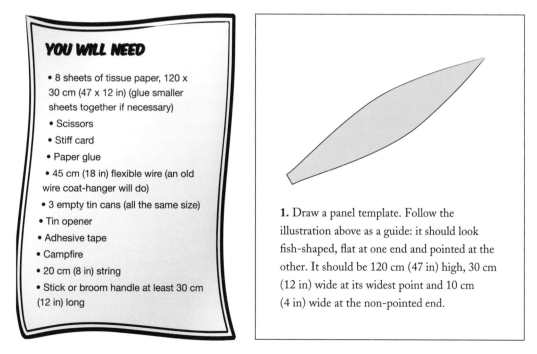

1. Draw a panel template. Follow the illustration above as a guide: it should look fish-shaped, flat at one end and pointed at the other. It should be 120 cm (47 in) high, 30 cm (12 in) wide at its widest point and 10 cm (4 in) wide at the non-pointed end.

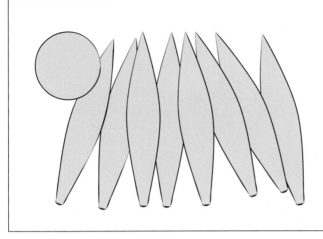

2. Using the panel template, draw and cut out eight tissue-paper panels. Cut out a small circle from the stiff card with a diameter of 10 cm (4 in).

3. Assemble two of your tissue-paper panels, folding the side of one over the other and gluing the overlap.

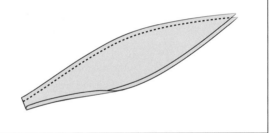

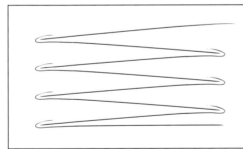

4. Continue to glue the rest of the panels in the same way (shown from above).

5. Glue the foldover of the last panel to the first panel, thus completing the circle.

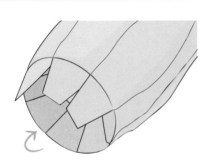

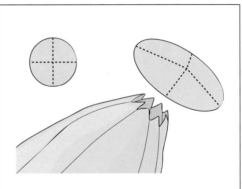

6. Twist your wire into a circle about 10 cm (4 in) in diameter – big enough to fit 2 cm (¾ in) inside the wide end of the balloon. Now make 2 cm (¾ in) deep notches at the base of each of the eight seams. Fold the resulting flaps over the wire and glue to secure them to the inside of the balloon.

7. Take your card circle and fold it in half and then in half again. Glue along the creases and around the edge of the circle, then apply it to the centre of the top of the deflated balloon, to form a crown.

TIP

If you find air is leaking from your balloon or it becomes damaged in flight you can easily repair it by gluing tissue paper over the affected area.

8. With a tin opener, remove both ends from three empty cans, tape them together and carefully place this 'stovepipe' in the campfire, ensuring that the pipe is steady and that the fire's flames have died down.

9. Tape a small loop of string to the top of the balloon and hook a stick or broom handle through the loop. Use this to hold the neck of the balloon over the pipe. As the balloon fills with hot air, it should inflate and begin to lift. When you feel it trying to ascend, remove the stick and let it fly into the air.

MAKE YOUR OWN WINDMILL

A SELF-MADE windmill provides a simple and delightful diversion on a balmy summer's day. Not only is it a 'breeze' to make, but it will provide an interesting and relaxing addition to your garden.

YOU WILL NEED

- 70 x 30 cm (28 x 12 in) sheet of 4 mm (¹/₈ in) thick plywood
- Saw
- Cylindrical piece of wood, about 15 cm (6 in) in diameter and 1.5 cm (¹/₂ in) thick
- Drill
- Vice
- Small screwdriver or chisel
- Screws (one with washer)
- Broom handle or similar pole, about 1 m (3 ft) long, cut into two equal lengths
- Glue

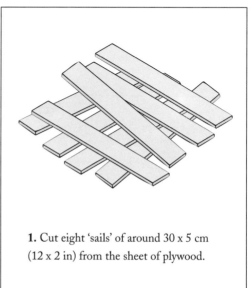

1. Cut eight 'sails' of around 30 x 5 cm (12 x 2 in) from the sheet of plywood.

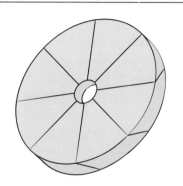

2. Draw a line through the middle of one of the flat circular faces of your cylinder of wood. Draw another line at right angles to this to divide the circle into four and twice more to divide the circle into eight equal sections. Drill a small hole in the exact centre of the circle where the lines intersect. Then turn the wood on its side and make a mark 1.5 cm (½ in) to the right of each of the eight lines on the opposite edge. Join up these points with a diagonal line.

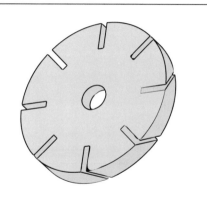

3. Place the cylinder in your vice. Saw along each diagonal line and again to its left, to create a slot about 5 mm (¹/₅ in) wide and 2.5 cm (1 in) deep. If necessary, clear the wood from the gap with a screwdriver or chisel.

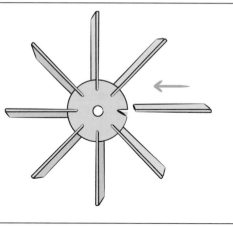

4. Fit each of the sails into the slots and secure using glue.

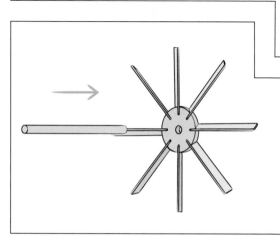

5. Push a screw with a washer through the hole in the circle of wood and then place another washer on the other side of the hole. Screw it into the end of one half of the pole, but not too tight or it will stop the sails from rotating freely.

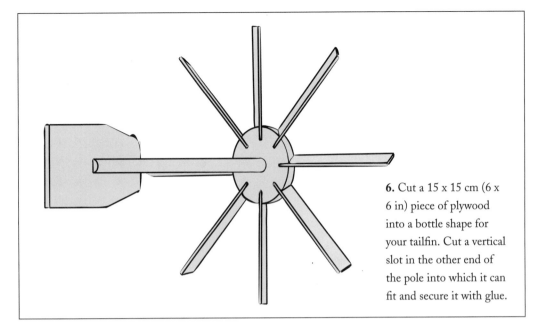

6. Cut a 15 x 15 cm (6 x 6 in) piece of plywood into a bottle shape for your tailfin. Cut a vertical slot in the other end of the pole into which it can fit and secure it with glue.

7. Hold the windmill with your right hand and balance the pole on your left index finger. Move your finger along the pole until you find its balancing point. Mark and drill a small hole through the pole. Now lightly screw it to the remaining length of pole, ensuring it can rotate on the support.

TIP

If you intend to leave your windmill outside for any length of time, it will be worth varnishing all your wooden pieces before assembly, as this will help protect your model from the effects of weathering.

MAKE A SLEDGE

SLEDS, sledges, sleighs or toboggans – whatever you like to call them, they're what winter was made for. The perfect vehicle for cross-country adventures, they can give unadulterated pleasure when you career down a hill or they may be the most practical means of dragging your pack along snow-packed lanes.

YOU WILL NEED

- Saw
- Drill
- Screwdriver and screws
- Wood glue
- Sandpaper
- Pair of old skis or 2 pieces of wood 215 x 8 x 8 cm (84 x 3 x 3 in) for the runners
- 8 pieces of wood 8 x 8 x 3.5 cm (3 x 3 x 1¼ in) for the runner blocks
- 5 floorboards (or 4 if you're using skis) 175 x 8 x 2 cm (69 x 3 x ¾ in)
- 5 pieces (or 4 if you're using skis) of wood 45 x 8 x 2 cm (18 x 3 x ¾ in) for the floor supports
- 1 piece of wood 50 x 8 x 2 cm (20 x 3 x ¾ in) for the pushing handle
- 2 pieces of wood 200 x 8 x 2 cm (79 x 3 x ¾ in) for the arm rests
- 2 pieces of wood 30 x 8 x 2 cm (12 x 3 x ¾ in) for the front uprights
- 2 pieces of wood 52 x 8 x 2 cm (20½ x 3 x ¾ in) for the short centre upright
- 2 pieces of wood 74 x 8 x 2 cm (29 x 3 x ¾ in) for the long centre upright
- 2 pieces of wood 96 x 8 x 2 cm (38 x 3 x ¾ in) for the rear upright
- Rope (around 1 m/3 ft)

Note: For the runners and blocks use hardwood, such as ash, oak, maple or hickory, as it will withstand the weather much better, but for the other parts you can use any kind of wood.

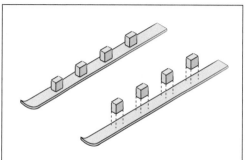

1. If you're able to get hold of a pair of old downhill skis to use as runners you will be at a great advantage. If you can't you can use wood – about 8 cm (3 in) thick – and cut a diagonal at the front to streamline your progress through the snow. To assemble the runners mark where your blocks will fit on the runners (two screws per runner) and drill small pilot holes. From the underside of the runners, screw each of the blocks in place.

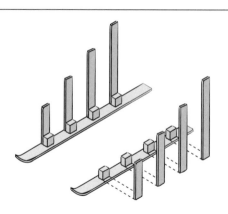

2. Ensuring they progress in height order (the lowest at the front), attach the uprights to the outer side of the runner blocks, fastening them with glue and two screws per joint. Leave the heads of the uprights squared up until you attach the arm rests.

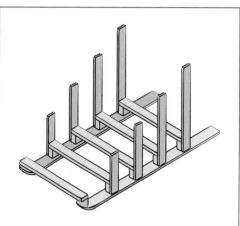

3. Now join together the runner blocks on each of the runners with the five floor supports (if you are lucky enough to have skis as runners, don't worry about the front support). Fasten them using glue and two screws per joint.

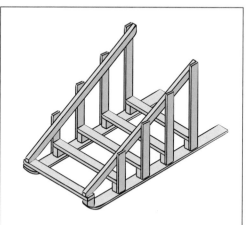

4. Screw and glue the arm rests into place and then trim the uprights at a diagonal, so they don't extend higher than the arm rests. Then trim the arm rests to ensure they sit flush with the rear upright.

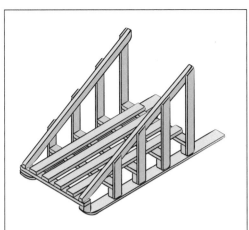

5. Space out your floorboards on the supports evenly and glue or screw them into place.

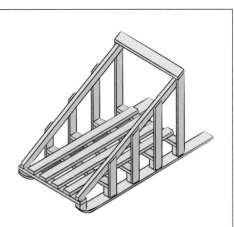

6. The pushing handle is the one piece that you should sand well before fixing to the sled to avoid suffering cuts and splinters when you're pushing. Glue and screw it across the back upright.

7. Drill a hole big enough for your tow rope through the first and fourth floorboards, behind the front floor support. Thread the rope through each of the holes and knot underneath to prevent the rope from slipping back.

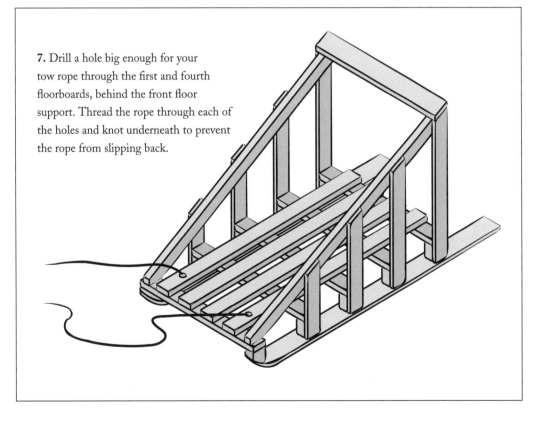

EXTREME
SURVIVAL

LIGHT A FIRE WITHOUT MATCHES

THE wilderness survivor may be able to get by without fire, but his life will be a great deal more comfortable with it. Making fire in the same fashion as our primitive ancestors is a fantastic way of journeying back in time, but it's also a skill that will certainly come in handy if you ever find yourself bereft of matches.

You can try creating a spark by hammering a flint or setting tinder alight by using a magnifying glass to concentrate the rays of the sun on to it, but the bow/drill method illustrated below is one of the most reliable means of making fire. Once you're familiar with the technique, the flames should flicker up pretty quickly.

YOU WILL NEED

- Couple of branches from a healthy, living tree – cedar, larch, sycamore, willow and poplar are particularly effective
- Sharp knife
- About 1 m (3 ft) of 1 cm (1/3 in) thick string (in an emergency use a shoelace)
- Soap
- Tinder bundle – a fist-sized, loosely packed 'bird's nest' of dry grasses, leaves and inner bark

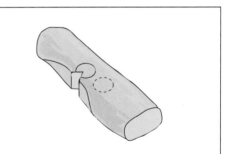

1. Create a fireboard from a branch that's about 20 x 10 cm (8 x 4 in) and 2 cm (¾ in) thick. Flatten the top and bottom and ensure it won't wobble when in use. Cut a notch as shown in the diagram and hollow out a small hole to receive your coal.

2. To make the bow, take a branch about the width of your forearm. It should be fairly rigid and only have a slight curve in it. Now take your string, which should be about one and a half times the length of your bow, and fix it to both ends of the bow, either by drilling a hole and passing the string through, making a small split in the wood, or wrapping it around the end. Secure with a fast knot, but keep the string fairly loose for now as you can always adjust it later.

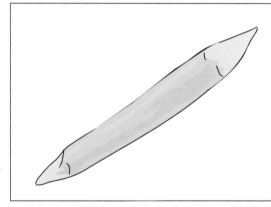

3. For the drill find a 30 cm (12 in) long section of branch and whittle it into a 2 cm (¾ in) thick straight drill with sharp points at each end. It will need to be lubricated with soap.

4. The socket is made from a section of the branch that's about 12 cm (4¾ in) long. Find a comfortable surface for gripping and gouge a hole 1 cm (¹/₃ in) deep in the middle. Make the sides of the hole slope in at a 45-degree angle, so you have a cone-shaped depression. The hole should be deep enough to keep the drill from slipping out and wide enough so that the drill edges won't touch the handhold except at the very tip.

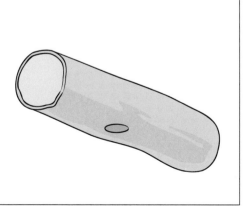

5. Place the fireboard on wood or stones so that it's stable and raised away from the ground slightly. Place your left foot across the fireboard with your instep just next to the cut hole. Load the drill by wrapping the string around it, then put the socket over the top of it. Hold the drill in your right hand and the socket in your left. The bow should be on the outside of the spindle, away from your left shin.

6. Press the socket gently down on the drill and draw the bow backwards and forwards, so that the drill turns. Gradually increase the downward pressure on the socket and push and pull the bow faster until the fireboard begins to smoke.

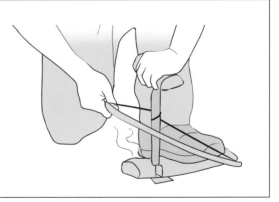

7. Continue to rotate the drill as the board begins to smoke and the char dust ignites into an ember. Transfer the glowing ember to a tinder bundle. Blow softly into the tinder bundle until you can see proper flames and then carefully transfer it to your fire.

MAKE A BIRCH BARK TORCH

NIGHT-TIME in the wilderness can be truly dark – and with no torch to light your way, your ability to travel or explore is severely limited. A birch bark torch, however, is a simple and effective means of producing enough light to find your path, to discover a suitable spot to shelter or even to hunt.

Caution: This is an extreme survival skill – stripping bark can damage a tree and permission should always be sought before attempting to collect the bark.

YOU WILL NEED

- Strips of bark
- Sharp knife
- String, vines or other binding material
- Campfire or matches

TIP

Although birch bark is the traditional material used in survival torches, you can experiment with other barks such as poplar or hickory. The best time to collect the bark is in spring or early summer, when the bark is of better quality and comes away easily from the tree.

1. Birch bark can be removed from the trunk or branches, living or recently dead, by making a vertical incision and cutting a slit down through the bark.

2. Use your knife to prize the bark away from the tree and gently strip it away from the wood. You will need a strip about 10–15 cm (4–6 in) wide.

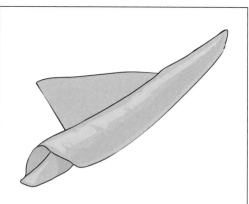

3. Place your strip of bark on the ground with the outside of the bark facing upwards. Take a corner of the bark and roll the strip so the inner bark forms the outside of the torch. Roll it as tightly as you can and at a slight angle to form a cone, making sure that the torch is a tube that you can see right through from one end to the other.

4. Now take whatever binding material you have handy – a vine will work as well as string. Starting at the thick end, which will be the top, lash the torch with three or four turns every 10 cm (4 in), leaving enough room to grasp as a handle at the bottom. Secure the binding with a clove hitch (see page 96).

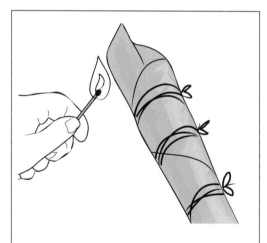

5. Now carefully light your torch by placing a match or a burning stick on the uppermost tip of it.

6. Hold your torch vertically, as this will keep it burning for longer and allow you to stay alert to any burning pieces of bark that may fall from the torch. If you find you need more light at any time, just blow gently at the burning end and the torch will flare up.

PIT COOKING

T HE idea of pit cooking conjures up images of primitive man preparing a huge beast for the whole tribe, yet, this form of cooking is still used today – especially for hog roasts! You can cook almost anything in a pit and the principle can be adapted to prepare a meal for large or small groups, or even individuals.

YOU WILL NEED

- Spade or other digging tools
- Armload of fibrous plants
- Rocks
- Campfire
- Brushwood and small pieces of wood
- Something to cook
- Pieces of heavy wood

1. Dig a hole in the ground about 1 m (3 ft) deep. The size of the hole should be about 50 cm (20 in) larger than the food you intend to cook. (A hole for a meal for two people should be about 30 cm/12 in wide). Keep the soil you take out of the ground to hand, as you'll need it later.

2. Gather your cooking materials. You will need about an armload of plants – fibrous plants such as grass or seaweed are most effective – and five rocks, each about the size of your head, per person. Try to find rocks that are as heavy and smooth as possible, as these are less likely to explode when heated.

3. Now build your campfire (see page 30) as close as possible to the pit, and light it. When it is burning well, position your rocks around the edge of the tepee structure.

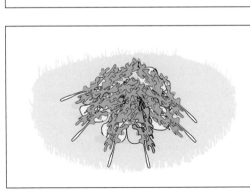

4. Cover the rocks and the fire with a layer of brushwood.

5. Place small pieces of wood over the brushwood, so that the rocks are completely covered. Now leave them to 'cook' for 90 minutes or more. **Caution:** The rocks can explode while they're heating up, so ensure they are fully covered, but always exercise great caution when dealing with red-hot rocks.

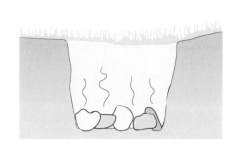

6. Carefully move half of your red-hot rocks and any burning wood around them into the bottom of the pit.

7. Working quickly at this point so that the rocks don't lose their stored heat, cover these rocks with a 30 cm (12 in) layer of the fibrous plants.

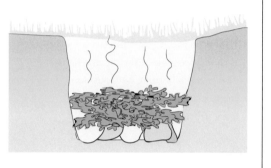

8. Place the elements of your meal – fish, meat or vegetables – on this bed of packed foliage. If you're cooking a large animal, such as a hog, place hot rocks in its body cavity and prop its mouth open with an apple to let the heat through.

9. Cover the food with a layer of fibrous grasses and plants as before.

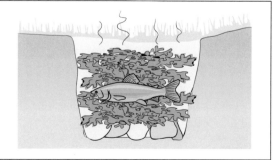

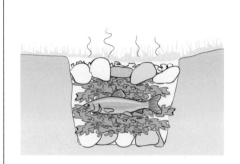

10. Gently toss the rest of the rocks and burning wood over the plants.

11. Now find something to cover the whole thing. A few pieces of heavy wood or some more large rocks should do the trick.

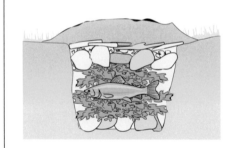

12. Move the soil that you originally dug out back over the pit so absolutely no steam or smoke can escape from around the edges. By covering the pit you maintain a constant temperature that's perfect for cooking.

13. Now leave the heat to do the work, letting it cook for 30 minutes for every 1 kg (2 lb) of food (this could mean over 24 hours to cook a whole hog!). When your calculations indicate the food should be done, dig it out carefully and take a look at it. If it's cooked, serve it up. However, if your meal hasn't cooked through, don't risk food poisoning. You may need to refill the pit with hot rocks, seal it up again and cook the food for a while longer.

MAKE A SPOON

T HE humble spoon can prove invaluable to the backwoodsman. The most practical and useful utensil to make – try eating your soup with a fork! – it's also a fun activity to engage upon when sitting around the campfire and will provide an excellent souvenir of your adventure.

YOU WILL NEED

- Piece of wood about 20 cm (8 in) long with a diameter of 4–5 cm (1 1/2–2 in) – almost any kind will do, but cedar, horse chestnut, willow and elm are good
  - Sharp knife
  - Small stone
- Hammer
- Campfire
- Small twig
- Sandpaper

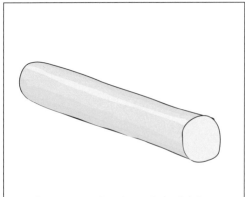

1. Cut your wood to size and check it has no cracks or large knots in it.

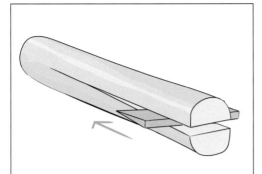

2. Make a notch about 5 mm (¼ in) deep through the centre of one end of the wood. Place a small stone in the groove as a wedge and hit it with the hammer to split the wood in half.

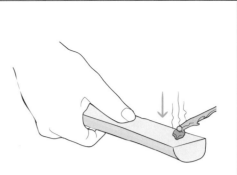

3. Carefully take a small ember from the campfire and place it on one end of the flat part of the wood. Use a small twig to hold the ember in place.

4. Gently blow, in a slow and steady manner, on the ember. It should glow and burn into the wood.

5. As the ember burns away the wood, move it around with the twig to give the desired size and shape to the bowl of the spoon.

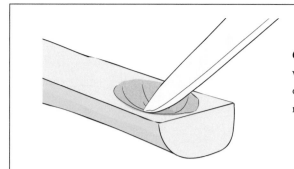

6. Using a knife, clean out all the charred wood. If the bowl is not deep enough or big enough, take another ember and repeat the process.

7. Once the bowl has the dimensions you desire, use your knife to carve and shape the inside and outside of the bowl end of the spoon.

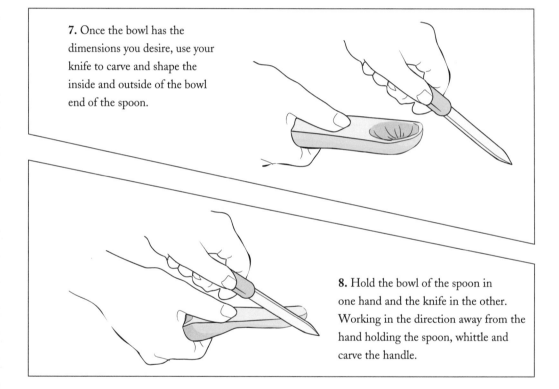

8. Hold the bowl of the spoon in one hand and the knife in the other. Working in the direction away from the hand holding the spoon, whittle and carve the handle.

9. Finally, use sandpaper to make the spoon smooth. If you don't have any sandpaper, rub some sand or shale across the spoon.

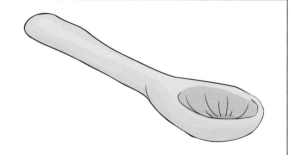

MAKE A FLINT KNIFE

THIS is the most basic and primitive tool of all, yet it can be a life-safer for any fellow trying to get by in the wilderness. Indeed, by making your own knife, you are taking the first step towards ensuring your own survival.

YOU WILL NEED

- Flint, about 3 x 1 cm (1 ¼ x ⅓ in)
- Piece of wood about 20 cm (8 in) long and as thick as your finger – look for green willow or other tough, flexible wood
- Twig
- String or tape

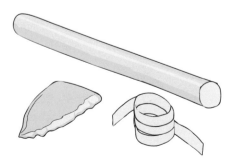

1. Take the flint in your hand and use it to carve a notch in the end of the piece of wood.

2. Split the wood three-quarters of the way down as shown in the illustration. Don't worry if the wood splits in half, as it will still be useable.

3. Insert a twig in the split to act as a wedge.

4. Bind the wood below the wedge while keeping tight hold of the tail of the string or tape.

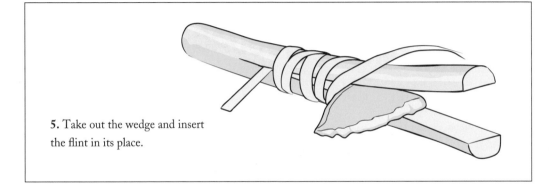

5. Take out the wedge and insert the flint in its place.

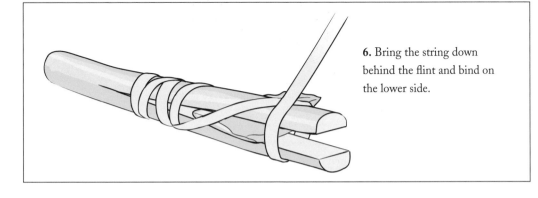

6. Bring the string down behind the flint and bind on the lower side.

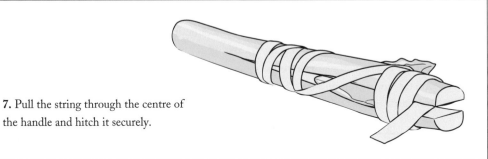

7. Pull the string through the centre of the handle and hitch it securely.

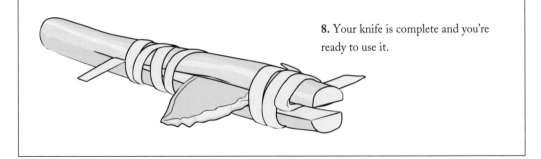

8. Your knife is complete and you're ready to use it.

BUILDING A BIVOUAC

THE two most important things that you need when you find yourself stranded somewhere in the great outdoors are water and shelter. However, the two don't necessarily go together very well!

You need to keep the water out of any shelter you build at all costs. Nothing will spoil a good night's sleep more than waking up to find yourself soaked to the bone. To make sure you get all the beauty sleep you need, you not only have to make your shelter, bivouac or "bivvy" as watertight as you possibly can, but you also have to consider the site on which you build it very carefully. Time spent creating a leak-free roof is completely wasted if you have located your bivvy on the bank of a river that decides to rise earlier than you do and join you inside. Choose as sheltered a spot as you can find, with no danger of any standing or running water invading your bivvy. As with any other kind of campsite, be careful to avoid danger areas such as clifftops, areas of fallen trees (you never know when another one might come down), slopes that show evidence of mudslides or avalanche, or obvious animal trails – goats, cattle or deer will eat your bivvy; lions, tigers or bears will eat you.

Your bivvy must be able to protect you not only from the rain or the snow but also from the other elements, such as the sun, the wind and the cold. In temperate regions, it is usually easy enough to find the sorts of material you will need to build a basic shelter. A few fallen logs for walls with some plastic sheeting, turf or foliage secured over them as a roof can form a rudimentary but effective shelter.

YOU WILL NEED

- 6 x 2m (6ft 6in) long, straightish, bendy branches
- 24 or more thinner, pliable branches (as long as possible)
- Lots of leafy twigs and foliage
- Cord or twine
- Sharp knife

1. Push the six branches into the ground in a circular pattern. bend them inwards, lashing them together in the middle. This will form the wall and roof frame of your bivvy.

2. Weave the twenty-four plus sticks horizontally in and out of the main frame in order to create a kind of loose basketwork effect all the way around your bivvy. Make sure that you leave a space low down between two of the frame branches. This will be your doorway, so choose a gap that faces away from any prevailing wind. Start at the bottom and work your way up to the top, keeping each horizontal level as close to the previous one as the available material allows. However, be careful not to get them too close together, because not only will you find yourself running out of the cross-weave sticks very quickly but you may also make the next stage much more difficult for yourself.

3. Weave your foliage into your basketwork "tent". Again, begin at the bottom. Keep the glossy or top side of the foliage facing outwards and pointing downwards so that any water will run off. Once you have completed one layer all the way around, the next layer has to overlap, just like the slates on the roof of a house. This keeps your bivvy as rain-proof as possible.

BUILD AN IGLOO

MANY people of the Arctic region spend their lives living in igloos made of snow and ice, because they are easy to build and they keep the body warm. Snow is a good insulator, so your body heat is trapped inside the igloo. They are the ideal shelter for a cold climate survivor.

1. Find a hard field of snow. Select a position for your igloo and the quarry area for your snow blocks. The depth of the snow on the site of the igloo should be at least 1 m (3 ft). Stamp down the area for your intended snow block quarry heavily for at least 15–30 minutes and then let it rest for 30 minutes.

YOU WILL NEED

- Snow
- Small axe
- Another person

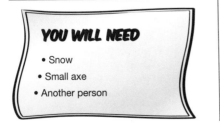

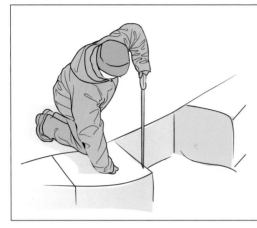

2. When the snow quarry is ready, start by making your snow blocks. They should be approximately 45 x 35 cm (18 x 14 in) and 20 cm (8 in) thick and then progressively add another 5–10 cm (2–4 in) to their height. They should be solid enough to be carried horizontally without breaking on account of their own weight. You will probably need around 50 blocks in total.

3. In the snow, draw a circle the size you want your igloo to be, taking into consideration how many people will need to sleep comfortably inside it.

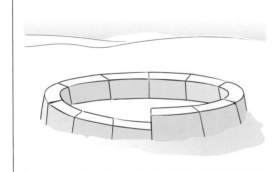

4. Start, logically enough, with the base layer of the igloo. One person should work on the outside, positioning the blocks around the perimeter of the circle. The other should work on the inside, constantly adjusting the blocks. The first block shouldn't be very tall, but each succeeding block should be a little taller, to form a gradually rising base. Always place the blocks topside up so that the original bottom of one block sits on the original topside of the blocks beneath. This helps the blocks to stick together. As each block is put in place, trim the adjoining surfaces with a knife.

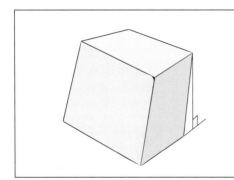

5. The second row of blocks should be bevelled at the bottom so the layer begins to slant inwards towards the middle.

6. The person inside must work carefully to prevent the blocks from falling; but after three or so rows are in place they should stand up by themselves. Continue to work upwards until the dome starts to form and the igloo is about shoulder-height.

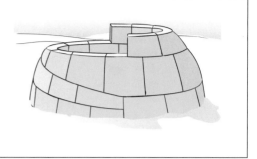

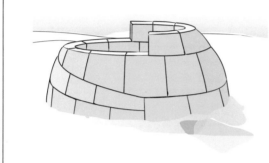

7. Dig out the floor of the igloo so it's a metre (3 ft) or so below the original surface level, and keep removing the snow that piles up inside. Now prepare your entrance, digging from a hole outside up into the igloo. Keep it as small as you can and be prepared to wriggle in.

8. Continue building the wall and as they get higher the blocks should angle in towards the centre until all you have left is an opening in the middle of the roof. This should be the size of one or two blocks and you need to lay these horizontally to fill in the hole.

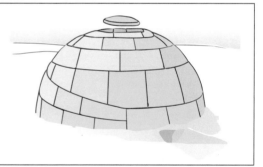

9. Now fill any cracks between blocks with snow and pack it in as tightly as possible.

CONSTRUCT A LOG RAFT

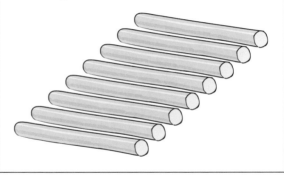

THE log raft has been a mainstay of outdoor adventure for generations. Sadly, we can't all live the life of Huckleberry Finn, but putting a raft together is a cinch for any group of lads bent on excitement.

YOU WILL NEED

- Axe
- Sharp knife
- Six 3 m (10 ft) long dry logs, about 30–40 cm (12–16 in) thick
- Four 2 m (6 ft 6 in) long logs, about 15 cm (6 in) thick
- 1 branch, as straight as possible and as tall as you
- Rope or vines for binding
- Grass and brush

1. Assemble all your materials on a dry bank of the river you intend to sail on. Use your axe to cut the logs to the correct lengths.

2. Lay all the larger logs side by side and make sure they fit snugly together. Run your axe across the logs to mark them about 20 cm (8 in) from each end. Now, separating them if it makes it easier, at both ends of each log, where you've made the marks, cut triangular notches about 10 cm (4 in) wide at the top, 20 cm (8 in) wide at the bottom and 10 cm (4 in) deep.

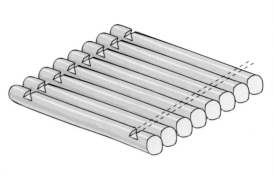

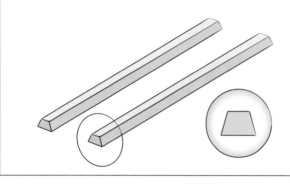

3. Now prepare two of the smaller logs to act as upper cross poles. Use your axe to hack them into trapezium-shaped pieces that will fit through the notches you have made.

4. Slide each of the cross poles through the notches to secure the logs, top and bottom. You may need to continue to shape them to make sure they fit easily, but don't worry if they sit a little proud of the raft platform.

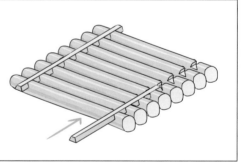

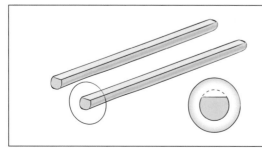

5. Take the other two small logs and, using the axe, roughly flatten one side.

6. Carefully turn the raft over ensuring the cross poles remain in the notches. Place the other two cross poles opposite them with the flattened sides downwards. Now lash them together, squeezing the raft in the middle.

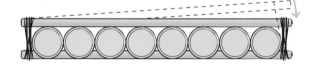

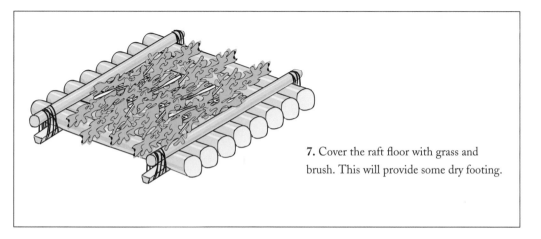

7. Cover the raft floor with grass and brush. This will provide some dry footing.

8. Strip your branch of any sharp knots or twigs – this will be your punting pole. Push your raft to the bank of the river. Take a firm grasp of the pole and push yourself into the water.

EVASION AND CAMOUFLAGE

YOUR outdoor pursuit games can be much more fun if you become adept at the art of becoming invisible. A fellow's eyes and ears are accustomed to picking out sudden noises, sharp movements and clashing colours, but in fact they can just as easily be fooled into thinking nothing is going on and no one is there at all.

SILHOUETTES

A human silhouette is an unmistakable shape to anyone surveying the landscape. If you need to walk near the top of a hill, then stay 5–10 m (15–30 ft) below the peak and if you have to climb over an obstacle, keep your body level with its top. Consider how your outline appears: secure branches to your clothes and headwear, keep your arms and legs close to your body and move in a crouch, gaining extra support by placing your hands on your knees.

MOVEMENTS

The ability to move without making any sudden movements or loud noises is essential to avoiding detection. When walking upright, your steps should be about half your normal stride. Lift the back foot to about knee-height and step forward to land lightly on the outside of the ball of the foot. Then roll off the edge of the foot on to the ball, putting down your heel, followed by your toes. Gradually shift your weight forwards to the front foot and start all over again. You should be able to stop at any point during the movement and hold that position as long as is necessary.

CRAWLING

If walking upright will give away your position, you can crawl on your hands and knees. Lower yourself until you're executing a modified push-up, with your body a few centimetres (inches) off the ground and your hands at chest breadth apart. Move yourself forward slightly and then lower yourself down to rest. Avoid dragging and scraping along the ground, as this makes excessive noise and leaves large trails for trackers to follow.

CAMOUFLAGE

Camouflage can help you blend in with your surroundings, but only if it's based on the vegetation and colours in your locale. Camouflage material should involve several similarly coloured patches mixed together in a pattern that hides the outline of the face or the body. Cover all areas of exposed skin, including your face, hands, neck and ears, using natural or man-made materials, including face paints, charcoal, mud, grass or leaves. Use the basic colours you see in the area and choose an appropriate pattern as illustrated.

Slash

Blotches

AREA	CAMOUFLAGE STYLE
Temperate deciduous forest	Blotches
Coniferous forest	Broad slash
Jungle	Broad slash
Desert	Slash
Arctic	Blotches
Grass or open area	Slash

SEA SURVIVAL

FOR all the fun that can be had at sea, it can be a terrifying environment when it turns against you. It's possible, however, to survive against the odds – the books are full of chaps who have been adrift at sea for weeks and lived to tell the tale. Here are a few survival tips if you're ever shipwrecked or fall overboard…

FLOATING ON YOUR BACK

If you find yourself in a dangerous situation in the water look for a safe place to head to – a buoy, a life raft, dry land or even a piece of floating debris that you can cling to. If there is nothing, then relax, as floating on your back uses up the least energy. Lie on your back in the water, spread your arms and legs, and arch your back. By controlling your breathing in and out, your face will always be out of the water and you may even be able to sleep in this position for short periods.

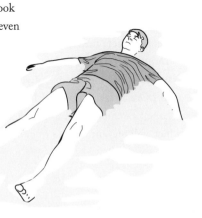

FLOATING UPRIGHT

If the sea is quite rough, it will be difficult to float on your back, but you can still float upright in the water. To master this technique, you need to take in air when your head is above water and then dip your face into the water. Bring your arms forward and relax until you need to take more air.

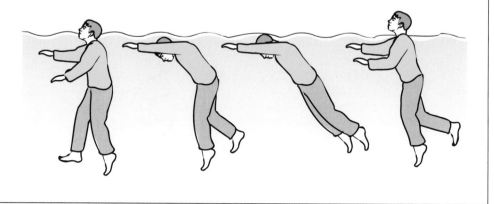

COLD WATER SURVIVAL

In very cold water of around 5°C (41°F) or less, don't remove clothing, except items that interfere with flotation, such as coats and boots, and don't tread water or exercise to keep warm. In fact don't swim at all unless you're forced to do so to get clear of danger or to stay afloat, and remember that even strong swimmers are unable to keep floating for more than a few minutes.

Do, however, face away from the waves to prevent the water splashing your face and adopt the HELP (Heat Escape Lessening Posture) position, which will prevent the loss of body heat (see right).

THE SURVIVAL MIRROR

Attracting the attention of aeroplanes and distant ships can be difficult in the vast expanses of an ocean, but a signal mirror has proved a lifesaver for many poor souls adrift at sea. The reflection can be effective at about 30 km (18 miles) surface to air and about 10–15 km (6–9 miles) surface to surface.

Hold your mirror close to your face or against your forehead and point the reflective surface towards the target that you are trying to signal to. Put your other hand in front of you, creating a 'V' with your fingers. Look through a hole or over the top of the mirror and focus the reflection of the sun on to your free hand. Then, using your 'V' as a sighting, aim it at your intended target area.

THE WHISTLE

A simple whistle could save your life if you're lost at sea, especially at night. It uses a small amount of energy compared to shouting and can be heard eight times further than the human voice, even above the roar of engines, breaking waves and thundering gale-force winds. You can use it to attract attention or give the international distress signal of six short blasts.

ESCAPE FROM QUICKSAND

WE'VE all seen the adventure movies where our hero strolls unwittingly into quicksand. Slowly dragged under, it looks like certain death until he effects a miraculous escape. Fortunately, being caught in real-life quicksand needn't be fatal and if you can swim in water you should be able to extricate yourself without undue tribulations.

Quicksand is a soupy mixture of sand and water that is usually found near flowing water, such as on a beach or riverbank. The sand becomes completely soaked by the water and is unable to drain away, and when you step on to the wet sand, the grains just slide past one another and you gradually slide under.

Unsurprisingly, the key is not to panic. The people who drown in quicksand are usually those who lose their cool and begin flailing their arms and legs about. If you do this, the quicksand reacts to your movements, so as you thrash around you create a vacuum and the sand is sucked in. Move slowly and the quicksand will change slowly, giving you time to react.

1. Quickly get rid of any weight you're carrying, such as a backpack, which might drag you down. Take off your shoes or boots if you're able, as they can create suction as you try to pull them out of the quicksand.

2. Focus on relaxing. Not only will breathing deeply help you remain calm, it will also make you more buoyant.

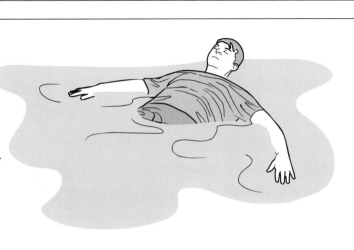

3. Try to bend backwards until you're floating on your back. The more you spread out your weight, the less likely you will be to sink.

4. Slowly bring your feet to the surface and 'swim' towards the side by making gentle paddling movements with your hands. This is the point where you need to be most patient. It could take more than an hour to reach the side, so don't exhaust yourself or try to swim quickly.

5. Don't be tempted to stand up as you approach firm land. Instead, remain lying down and roll from the quicksand on to solid ground.

WHAT TO DO IF YOU'RE CAUGHT IN AN AVALANCHE

BEING caught in an avalanche can be a terrifying ordeal and an experience that can cost you your life, but if you can keep your head at the moment of crisis, make sensible decisions and take appropriate action you will have a chance of survival.

SIGNS OF AN AVALANCHE

Most avalanches occur on slopes of between 30–45 degrees, but they can still happen on any slope given certain conditions. Here are some warning signs that should alert you to the risk.

- Large amounts of new snow – snowfalls of 20 cm (8 in) or more create the most hazardous situations, while falls of over 10 cm (4 in) still pose some threat.
- High winds, particularly overnight, or evidence of recent wind activity, such as cornices.

- Cracks in the snow.
- Creaking noises or a hollow-sounding snow surface.
- The sound of dripping water or balls of wet snow running down the slope.
- A heavy thaw or sudden rise in temperature.

If in doubt, return to a safe area immediately as your life could be at risk.

HOW TO GIVE YOURSELF A GOOD CHANCE OF SURVIVING

1. Turn your back to the avalanche. Shout a warning to any other people in the area – this will also alert them to your position – and then close your mouth tightly.

2. Remove any and all cumbersome items such as your backpack, skis and ski poles. Try to get out of the main path of the avalanche and, if possible, grab hold of a tree or a bush. An avalanche may move at more than 80 kph (50 mph) so you won't be able to outrun it.

3. Once you're in the midst of the avalanche try to 'swim' to the edge of it, but with, not against, the flow of the snow. Keep your head upslope and your feet downslope, and thrust up towards the surface.

4. If the snow covers you, hold your hands in front of your face and push out to make breathing space. Move your head from side to side to give yourself some room to breathe.

5. When you feel you've come to a halt, reach upwards and try to leave one hand above the snow. Being able to wave your hand or even fingers will make it easier for rescuers to find you.

6. If you can't reach outside air in an arm's length then don't attempt to dig your way out as you'll only waste precious air and energy. Instead curl into a foetal position and protect as much of your body as possible. Cup your hands over your face allowing clear space between your hands and face as this will keep the snow out of your face and mouth and, again, provide you with some breathing room.

POISONOUS SNAKES AND HOW TO AVOID THEM

SNAKES are one of the outdoors' great hazards. You don't need to be an extreme explorer to encounter a snake and indeed they can be difficult to avoid. Many of these critters are harmless, but it's not wise to creep too near, just in case you discover you're dealing with one of nature's master assassins!

AVOIDING SNAKEBITES

- Leave snakes alone. Stay a couple of metres (yards) away and don't try to pick them up or handle them. Sometimes even dead snakes can still deliver a bite.
- If you encounter a snake, stand completely still – snakes predominantly attack moving targets.

- Check for snakes before putting your hands into dark places, such as rock crevices, heavy brush or hollow logs.
- When walking through long grasses, wear hiking or heavy walking shoes.
- Look before you step, and beat and bash with a long branch or stick three to five paces ahead of you.

TREATING A SNAKEBITE

- Get the victim away from the snake and into a safe area.
- NEVER try to suck out the venom by mouth.
- Calm the victim down and keep them still.
- Lie the victim down and keep the affected limb lower than the heart.
- Remove any jewellery that may constrict with swelling.
- If possible, wash the bite with soap and water.
- Apply a bandage 5–10 cm (2–4 in) above the bite (see below). The band should be loose enough to slip a finger under it and shouldn't cut off the flow of blood. Readjust the bandage if it tightens due to swelling.
- The victim should sit still for at least 20–30 minutes to let the venom localise.

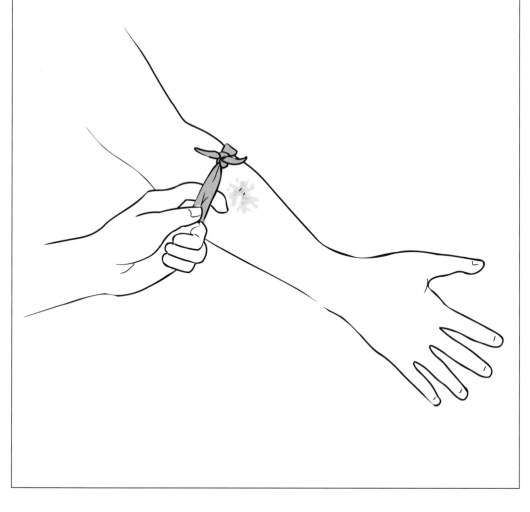

POISONOUS SNAKES

No single characteristic distinguishes a poisonous snake from a harmless one, except the presence of poison fangs and glands. The following, however, are some deadly snakes you might encounter…

American copperhead: these snakes are found in rocky, wooded and mountainous regions throughout the USA. They have a copper-coloured body that is criss-crossed with dark brown bands and are around 60 cm (24 in) long.

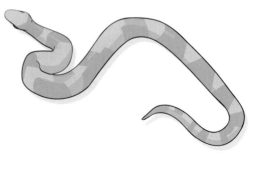

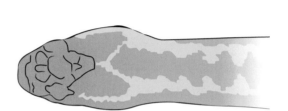

Rattlesnake: mainly found in the southwestern United States, rattlesnake species are identified by their jointed rattles on the tail. Before striking, the rattle emits a sizzling buzz.

Adder: the only poisonous snake native to Britain, adders are distinctively marked with a dark zigzag along the spine and an inverted 'V' on the neck. Adders prefer undisturbed countryside and are found in open woodland, hedgerows, sand dunes, riverbanks and bogs.

Cobra: the world's longest venomous snake, the cobra averages 3.7 m (12 ft) in length and is found throughout southern Asia and Africa. They can be identified by the hoods that they flare when angry or disturbed.

Tiger snake: an inhabitant of southern and eastern Australia, the tiger snake often has a striped marking and is around 1 m (3 ft) long. It feeds on frogs, fish, small birds and other small mammals, but will attack humans if disturbed.

Taipan: Australia's largest venomous snake, the olive brown Taipan can grow to 3 m (10 ft) in length. It has an extraordinarily fast and accurate bite, and allows its prey to escape and die before swallowing it whole.

POISONOUS INSECTS AND SPIDERS

BUGS and spiders are as much a part of the outdoor world as fresh air, beautiful scenery and exhilarating adventure – so get used to them. Most will just be annoying or give you an irritating itch, but, as you'll discover below, there are some members of this world it would be as well to avoid.

BITE OR STING?

A bite is when a creature injects venom through the mouth. Creatures that bite include spiders and ants. A sting is when the creature stings you with a stinger. Venomous insects, such as bees, wasps, scorpions and hornets, attack as a defence mechanism, injecting painful, toxic venom through their stings.

Avoiding insect bites

- Wear long-sleeved shirts and long trousers.
- Wear light-coloured clothes that make it easier to see insects on your clothes.
- Tuck your trousers into your socks.
- Wear a hat to keep insects out of your hair.
- As soon as you can, take a shower and check all over your body for ticks.
- Insects can bite at any time of day, but most bites occur in the evening, so extra vigilance is necessary after sunset.

BROWN RECLUSE SPIDER

Native to the midwestern and southern states of the USA, and recognizable by the dark violin-shaped mark on its head, the brown recluse is not aggressive, but if trodden on or squashed can deliver a seemingly innocuous bite that later becomes painful.

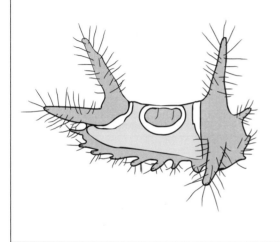

SADDLEBACK CATERPILLAR

About 2.5 cm (1 in) long, with an oval, purplish-brown 'saddle' in the middle of a green patch on its back, this caterpillar has four protruding poisonous horns and many smaller ones on the sides of its body.

KILLER BEE

These Africanized honey bees attack in greater numbers and with more aggression than common bees. They will chase a person for half a kilometre (a third of a mile) and will wait up to 30 minutes for someone taking refuge under water.

FUNNEL-WEB SPIDER

Probably the most poisonous spider in the world, these large, dark Australian spiders have venom to which humans are particularly susceptible. When approached, they rear up into a ready-to-strike position, displaying massive fangs which are so strong that they can penetrate a child's fingernail.

TARANTULA

The South American Goliath Tarantula has a body length of 12 cm (5 in) and a leg span of up to 30 cm (12 in), but they are relatively harmless to humans. Their bites are no worse than a bee sting and their hairs will just produce an annoying itch.

MOSQUITO

The blood-sucking mosquito can not only leave an irritating red rash, but in many tropical countries can be life-threatening, spreading diseases such as malaria, yellow fever and West Nile Virus. Especially dangerous is the aggressive Asian tiger mosquito, identifiable by its black and white striped legs; its rapid bite allows it to escape most people's attempts to swat it.

BLACK FLY

Sometimes called buffalo gnats, turkey gnats or white socks, these American and African blood suckers are fierce biters and spread several diseases, including river blindness in Africa. They usually bite during the day in outdoor shaded or partially-shaded areas and often strike where clothing – often dark blue – fits snugly against the body.

HOW TO WRESTLE A CROCODILE

FIRST things first. Getting anywhere near a crocodile is not something even the bravest of chaps should even consider. They are aggressive, incredibly strong and think nothing of tucking into a wayward trekker for elevenses. However, should the unthinkable occur, here are a few facts and techniques that might just stand you in good stead...

Crocodile attack facts:
- Crocodiles become more aggressive during the mating season.
- Crocodiles can move very quickly over short distances on land.
- Crocodiles tend to drag their prey under water and drown them.
- An attacking crocodile can perform a 'death roll', biting, gripping and then rapidly spinning its body to weaken its prey.

A crocodile can kill in just a few seconds, so bear in mind that you may not have time to read this sound advice during the actual conflict...

1. Crocodiles use a dangerous sideways lunge, so never engage them from the side. If you can, surprise them and approach them from behind.

2. Use both hands to grab the beast's neck. Keep a good grip behind the head, very close to its skull where the skin is the softest.

3. Now get your bodyweight on the croc's back. Spread your legs apart and position them across its torso, in front of its hind legs to avoid the whipping tail.

4. As you force the neck down the crocodile's jaws should close. Use your hands to keep them shut. Crocodiles have strong muscles for closing their jaws, but weaker ones for opening them, so use this to your advantage.

5. Slide your legs down the body until they are either side of the tail. Then grip firmly to stop the croc moving its tail and hold this position.

That's all there is to it! Now just wait to be rescued – or for the referee to declare you the winner!

ESCAPING A BEAR ATTACK

A CHANCE sight of a bear in the wild is an exhilarating experience. They really are fascinating and majestic creatures, but too close an encounter can also be terrifying. Powerful and aggressive, bears can easily maim or even kill a human. Thankfully, such bear attacks are rare, but here are some tips should you ever be hiking in bear country….

WHY DOES A BEAR ATTACK?

- If you come too close or between a female bear and her cubs – this is the cause of over three-quarters of bear attacks.
- If the bear is surprised, or startled.
- If a human gets too close to a bear's food supply.
- If a hungry bear is looking for food.

HOW TO AVOID ENCOUNTERS WITH BEARS

- Advertise your presence when in bear country - talk loudly, sing, or carry cow bells. Bears are reclusive creatures and will seek to avoid you.
- Be careful with food smells. Don't cook close to camp and store all foods in plastic at least 100 metres (yards) from camp.
- Watch for fresh bear tracks or droppings on the trail or near your camp.
- If you find a dead animal carcass, leave the area immediately. Bears often feed on a carcass for days.

ENCOUNTERING A PREDATORY BEAR

If the bear attacks your camp in the night, it is almost certainly looking for a midnight snack. It is probably hungry and desperate. In this case you will have no option but to fight: use your spray, punch and kick and use any available object as a weapon. If it is a black bear rather than a grizzly, you may have some luck if you strike it in the eyes or on the snout.

ENCOUNTERING A DEFENSIVE BEAR

1. If the bear has not seen you, walk away calmly and quietly.
2. Do not be alarmed if the bear stands up on its hind legs, it is just trying to get a better look and smell.
3. If the bear sees you, DO NOT run or try to climb a tree. Bears can do both of these quicker and more effectively than you.
4. DO NOT maintain eye contact with the bear, instead speak to it in a low, calm voice and slowly retreat.
5. If you have a backpack, keep it on. It may offer some body protection
6. If you have a Bear Deterrent Pepper Spray, you should have it to hand and know how to use it. If the bear charges, you will need to spray at its face or spray a cloud out in front of it
7. If the bear charges at you, stand tall, speak louder (but still calmly), and wave your arms around to make yourself look bigger. Sometimes a bear will bluff charge several times and still eventually turn away.
8. If the bear makes contact with you, immediately play dead. Lie flat on the ground and do not struggle. Put your hands behind your neck and curl up in a foetal position with your legs tucked in.
9. The bear should now leave you alone. Continue to lie still for at least 20 minutes – a bear may return if it sees you moving.

RESOURCES

BOOKS

Scouting for Boys: A Handbook for Instruction in Good Citizenship by Robert Baden-Powell, Oxford University Press.

The Scout's Companion by Sonja Patel, Think Publishing Limited.

Woodcraft by "Nessmuk", Dover Publications Inc.

Green Woodworker's Pattern Book: Over 300 Traditional Craft Designs by Raymond Tabor, B.T. Batsford Ltd.

The Poacher's Handbook by Ian Niall, Merlin Unwin Books.

The Backpacker's Cookbook by David Coustick, Neil Wilson Publishing.

The Campfire Cookbook: Recipes for the Outdoors by Don Philpott and Pam Philpott, Collins & Brown.

Home Tree Home: "the Principles of Treehouse Construction" and Other Tall Tales by Peter Nelson, Penguin Books Australia Ltd.

Bushcraft: Outdoor Skills and Wilderness Survival by Mors Kochanski, Lone Pine Publishing, Canada.

Bushcraft: An Inspirational Guide to Surviving the Wilderness by Raymond Mears, Hodder & Stoughton Ltd.

Bushcraft Survival by Raymond Mears, Hodder & Stoughton.

Trapper's Bible: Traps, Snares and Pathguards by Dale Martin, Paladin Press.

SAS Survival Handbook: How to Survive in the Wild, in Any Climate, on Land or at Sea by John Wiseman, Collins.

Compass and Map Navigator by Michael Hodgson, Globe Pequot Press.

Navigation for Walkers by Julian Tippett, Cordee.

Learning to Sail: In Dinghies or Yachts – a No-nonsense Guide for Beginners of All Ages by Basil Mosenthal, Adlard Coles Nautical.

Sailing for Kids by Gary Kibble and Steve Kibble, Fernhurst Books.

Ice Skating: Steps to Success (Steps to Success Activity Series) by Karin Kunzle-Watson and Stephen J. DeArmond, Human Kinetics Europe Ltd.

Learn to Surf by James MacLaren, The Lyons Press.

Surfer's Start-up: Beginner's Guide to Surfing (Start-up Sports) by Doug Werner, Tracks Publishing, USA.

Anyone Can Be an Expert Skier: The New Way to Ski Bk 1 by Harald R. Harb, W. W. Norton & Co. Ltd.

Building an Igloo by Ulli Steltzer, Henry Holt & Company.

52 Decks: Fun Things to Do at the Beach by Lynn Gordon, Chronicle Books.

Sandcastles Made Simple: Step-by-Step Instructions, Tips and Tricks for Building Sensational Sand Creations by Lucinda Wierenga, Stewart, Tabori, & Chang.

The Kids' Building Workshop: 15 Woodworking Projects for Kids and Parents to Build Together by Craig Robertson, Barbara Robertson and J. Craig Robertson, Storey Publishing.

Carpentry for Children: Simple Step-by-step Plans for Great Do-It-Yourself Projects by Lester Walker, Overlook.

Nature's Playground: Activities, Crafts and Games to Encourage Your Children to Enjoy the Great Outdoors by Fiona Danks and Jo Schofield, Frances Lincoln Publishers.

Aircraft Workshop: Learn to Make Models That Fly (Learn to Make Models) by Kelvin Shacklock, Special Interest Model Books.

The Complete Knot Pack: A New Approach to Mastering Knots and Splices by Steve Judkins, Fernhurst Books.

The World's Most Dangerous Bugs (World's Top Tens) by Nick Healy, Edge Books.

Venomous Snakes of the World by Mark O'Shea, New Holland Publishers Ltd.

WEBSITES

Beach games
familyfun.go.com

Curling
www.englishcurling.org.uk
www.curlingbasics.com/

Dodgeball
The National Amateur Dodgeball Association:
www.dodgeballusa.com

Go-karts, sleds, etc.
http://www.vintageprojects.com

Hobbies and projects
http://www.boyslife.org/section/hobbies-projects/

www.projectsandhobbies.com
www.diynetwork.com

How to do just about anything
http://www.ehow.com

'How to' manual that anyone can write
http://www.wikihow.com

'How to' videos from experts
http://www.expertvillage.com

Ice skating
www.iceskating.org.uk
www.usfigureskating.org

Knots
www.animatedknots.com

Model gliders
www.guillow.com
balsa-models-planes.com

Outdoor activities for boys
http://www.inquiry.net

Rock climbing
www.ukclimbing.com

Sandcastles
www.sandcastlecentral.com

Scouting
www.usscouts.org
www.scouts.org.uk
www.scoutingresources.org.uk
http://www.scoutorama.com

Snakes
www.aboutsnakes.com

Spiders
www.termite.com/spider-identification.html
http://venomous-spiders.nanders.dk

Surfing
www.surfing-waves.com
www.santabarbarasurfing.com

Treehouses
www.treehouselife.co.uk
www.treehousemagazine.com

Water rockets
users.bigpond.net.au/mechtoys/waterrocket.html
http://www.uswaterrockets.com
http://www.geocities.com/yoramretter

Wilderness survival
http://www.wilderness-survival.net
http://www.outdoorlife.com
www.map-reading.com
www.mountainnature.com
www.survivaliq.com

INDEX